Anonymus

I awoke!

Conditions of life on the other side

Anonymus

I awoke!
Conditions of life on the other side

ISBN/EAN: 9783742837288

Manufactured in Europe, USA, Canada, Australia, Japa

Cover: Foto ©Thomas Meinert / pixelio.de

Manufactured and distributed by brebook publishing software
(www.brebook.com)

Anonymus

I awoke!

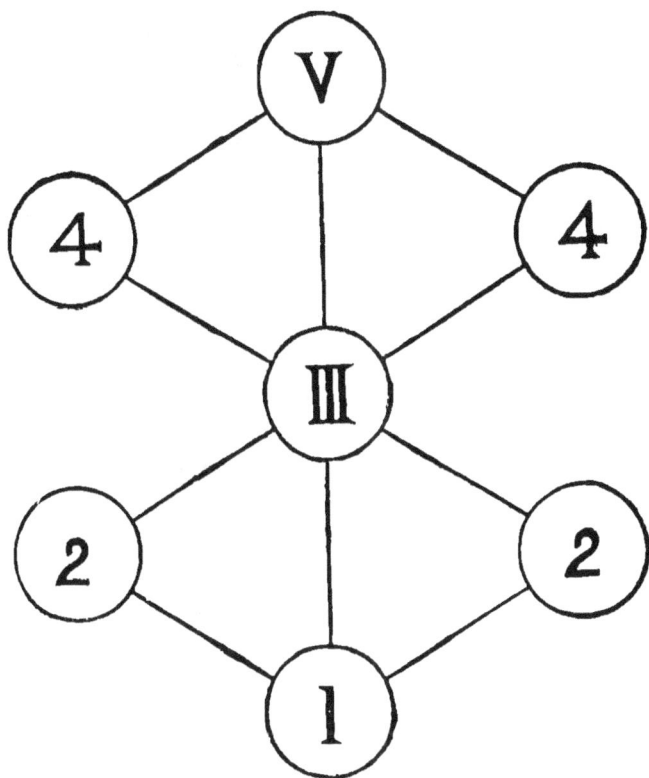

" I AWOKE ! "

Conditions of Life on the other Side

Communicated by Automatic Writing.

ENLARGED EDITION.

London:
DAVID STOTT, 370, OXFORD STREET, W.
1895.

PREFACE.

IT will hardly be necessary to explain to any reader what is meant by "Automatic Writing"; but as the *modus operandi* differs slightly with different people, it may be well to state precisely how this book was written.

Three friends, who had been receiving messages by this means on various subjects for some time, were told that they could have a connected account of the life on the other side—as far as such could be put into words—if they sat together occasionally for that purpose.

They accordingly met at various times and places— indoors or in the open air—always in broad daylight.

One of them, taking paper and pencil, would write rapidly for about twenty minutes without looking at the paper, and with no knowledge at the time of what was written. At the next sitting the thread would be taken up exactly where it had been dropped, no matter how long a time had elapsed between the sittings.

The book is presented exactly as it was received. It has needed no correction, and, with the exception of the title page, no word has been added, the headings, quotations, etc., all being given in the same way.

There have been various methods of explaining this automatic or unconscious writing ; but those to whom these messages have come believe that the simplest and most reasonable explanation is, that these communications come, as they profess to do, from those who once dwelt here, but have now passed over into the Unseen.

INDEX.

PART I.— THE PSYCHE.

PART II.—THE PNEUMA.

"I AWOKE!"

PART I.—THE PSYCHE.

INTRODUCTORY.

DEAR FRIENDS,— It has long been the wish of many on our side that we might be able to give to some in the land from which we have come, a more complete and connected account of our life and its conditions. We know, of course, that there have been revelations from our world to yours during the past ages ; and indeed, that there has never been an age without many such revelations. The great " Opening " that was given to John by the Master is doubtless the greatest of these ; but from the very circumstances under which it was given, it is perhaps the most difficult of comprehension. Our Master had passed rapidly through the intermediate or Hades state, and had entered into the heavenly sphere. There, when he had entered into the spirit of his new life, his heart turned naturally to the one among his earthly friends who best, and almost alone, could understand him, and he sought to reveal to John in a vision the things that he had just entered into, and which, to John, were things that would shortly come to pass. Such a vision John found well-nigh impossible to put into words, though his spirit comprehended it fully. Now we, dear friends, in our humble way, will strive to tell you things that must shortly come to pass ; and when we have to deal with heavenly things we will get those who dwell in the spheres to first tell us, and we will interpret them to you as well as we can.

There is no reason why the keys of Hades and of Heaven should not be put into your hands, for we believe that you have living faith, that faith which gives you the right to enter in and take possession.

You will, perhaps, ask in what manner we can communicate with you ; how do we give you these writings ? We are still earthly enough to be able to put our psycho-electric force into touch with your electric currents ; this touches your sub-conscious brain. We cannot actually see what we write, but we know that it is what we intended when it enters your conscious brain. The choice of words, the style, is greatly limited by your own powers, but not entirely ; we can sometimes use words and phrases with which you are unacquainted. Then as we progress here, and the spirit gradually dominates the soul, our power to give you words will fail ; we shall only reach you by the voiceless power of love and of sympathy, and our intercourse will be confined to that soul-raising influence which you call sometimes worship, sometimes ecstacy. When the Master had withdrawn from the psychic, he could only communicate with his friends by the spirit, and so it is with us all. When messages come with the names of those who have long passed over, it is either from one of their " school," or it has been passed through a medium on our side before it was sent on to you.

LIMITATIONS OF KNOWLEDGE, OF EXPERIENCE, AND OF POWER.

> " An infant crying in the night ;
> An infant crying for the light ;
> And with no language but a cry."

How absurd in the light of experience, seems the old belief that when a soul has passed " the article of death," immediately he attains all knowledge, power, and experience. Not only to us who have already passed, but to you with your truer knowledge of the slow and gradual development of all true life, will this idea seem most foolish. No, indeed, our knowledge is—though marvellously increased—still limited, and our powers yet in their childhood.

Yet, as having climbed some peaks that you have only dreamed of, we may impart something to you that shall be not only of interest to you now, but as a chart of the country when you come over.

In what position do we stand to you then? In the position of the " angels of the churches," spoken of by John. They were those who had passed over from your world into this, but had not yet reached that higher state where the Master was at that time. Still imperfect; full of faults, yet striving to grow towards perfection, they were aiding their brethren on earth as far as they could. We will try to be true and wise "angels" to you, and give you some of the results of our collective knowledge and experience. " He that hath ears to hear, let him hear what the ' angel' saith unto the churches."

Before trying to give you some of the phenomena of our life, it may be better to tell you something of our faith with regard to the great foundation principles of God, of man, and of human life.

THE UNITY OF GOD.

"Say unto the people, the I AM hath sent me unto you."
"Why enquirest thou after my name, seeing that it is
    hidden."
What is God?

Directly we use names or terms we limit the limitless; we define the indefinable. The use of names, where they are characteristic of the object, and not mere perfunctory terms without meaning, is to qualify. The name shows that the person possesses attributes different from those possessed by other persons, and implies that others possess attributes which he does not, and we therefore limit him to the extent of their attributes. If I call God "Father" I limit him so far that I imply He is not my brother, and if I call him "Lord," I imply that He is not my equal, my companion, my friend. All definitions, then, are limited, and, to a certain extent, misleading ; yet we must avail ourselves of some terms. The truest is that given through Moses—I AM. That is: I am all being, and all being is myself; yet even this seems to shut him out of phenomena. Yes, there is One and only One in the universe ; one in whom all being, all force, all phenomena are united, and beside this one there is no other ; there is no life that is not God, there is no death that is not God, no thing, no spirit ; all is one, and that one—for want of a better term—we speak of as God, while the very power with which we speak it is God ; the Absolute, the Limitless, the Infinite.

From this first principle will follow readily and reasonably the second—*e.g.*

THE UNITY OF MAN.

By this I mean, not the union of one man with another merely, not the homogeneity of the race, but the absolute unity of man with God as one in essential being, if not in present potentiality. We often say God created man. This is apt to produce a false impression, for we think of a creation of something out of nothing ; a beginning to be of man ; a separation of man from God, which is not really so. A clearer view may be got by thinking of God as breathing into the limited and time-and-space-bound-physical man the breath of his being—and man became. The eternal purpose that had always been and always would be, was thus manifested in phenomena, and became for a time subject unto bondage, that its full development might be attained by the fighting with that which seemed to be antagonistic to its divine nature.

" What is man that Thou art mindful of him ? " Ah! he is indeed Thyself, and thou God art myself ; I and He are one ; I came from God and I shall return to Him.

" Before Abraham was, I AM ": these are the words not only of the Master, but of us all : we too may say :

I AM:

I AM the Existent:

I AM the All-Inclusive:

I AM the Infinite.

THE UNITY OF LIFE.

From the two former propositions proceeds by necessity our third: *e.g.*, the unity of life. Here also we mean—not merely the union of one form of life with another, or the development of the higher from the lower—but its true unity with the one being which we have spoken of as God and as man.

(From the Chain of Life given at an earlier period.)

The absolute unity of life cannot be too strongly insisted upon. Life is one; it is an electrical, absolutely non-material stream of influence from the great source of life. It has not been, it cannot be discovered by the microscope, or the dissecting knife; it is not material, and cannot be revealed to material eyes; but it informs matter, and is manifested in and through it. If we think of the universe as a chain, it should be as of separate links strung together on an invisible string, and that string the breath of the Divine; without this breath the universe would immediately dissolve, and vanish from mortal eyes. In the beginning the earth was without form and void. In the beginning: that is when the Living One saw fit to bring into outward manifestation some of the thoughts of His heart, and into the chasm, the void space, he breathed the breath of His own being. Then the fluid, gaseous, invisible matter cohered by the power of this breath, and a solid earth arose where before was no such thing. (Of the actual origin of matter we know not yet, as we know not the origin of life, only its first manifestations.)

Life has, broadly speaking,. four forms of manifestation. First, The Unconscious; Second, The Conscious; Third, The Self-conscious;

Fourth, The God-conscious. Its lowest form may be seen in the bare granite; the second in vegetable life, the third in the animal, and the fourth in man. In these stages the creation is well spoken of in Genesis, that book which as an epitome of life can never be surpassed. Now these forms closely touch, and are inter-related to one another; there is no great chasm between each, and the life is essentially the same in all; in the lowest it is more motionless, more dormant, but as it rises in the scale its motion increases. Is it then the same life in me that is in the stone or the flower; in the wild beast or the singing bird? Yes, precisely the same, in greater fulness, or more highly developed, or in whatever way it may be expressed. As far as that side of you, your manifested being is concerned, you are absolutely at one with all nature. This life is ever seeking fresh manifestations; when driven from one form by the break of death, it seeks another, and pressed on by the will of its Father

it seeks constantly to manifest itself, and pulses
through the chain of the universe, flowing ever
round and round in great cycles from God to God.

"Not a sparrow falleth to the ground without
your Father:" thus spake one who knew.

Nothing is so relentless, so cruel, so pitiless
as Nature: she does not distinguish between
ignorance and sin, between the strong and the
helpless: all who transgress one of her immu-
table laws must pay the penalty, and probably
entail suffering on others: for the individual
she cares nothing, and but little for the type.
This is what the scientists say; is it true? Yes,
it is true; both sayings are true. How are they
to be reconciled? First; no destruction of life
is possible; it cannot be, it never is destroyed:
forms fall to pieces, but the life escapes and is
manifested in some other way. Stagnation is not
the best state: the rock may well envy the flower
that grows on its breast and lives (in that form)
but a little day: the flower may envy the bird

even if snared by the fowler: yet envy is not needed, and the life will pass in due time through all, from the lowest to the highest.

Second : Pain is caused by the conflict of the physical with the psychical ; sin by the conflict of the psyche with the pneuma. Both are real blessings, for they stir the forces into stronger and better action. When we pass over we leave the lower forms of life behind, taking only the higher, and are clothed upon with a body which is to yours as spirit to flesh, yet which is still a manifested form.

With regard to that fourth form of life which I have called the God-conscious, I do not imply by it an ordinary faith in a God ; the possession, or non-possession of such faith is a small matter. By God-consciousness I mean the power of worship, of faith in, and love for another, for the race : something higher than the affection of a dog for his master ; the power that can say : Let me perish, if through my loss others may gain.

Neither self, nor what self can give is the first thing, but a willing self-abnegation for the good of any.

This I call God-consciousness, as it is his leading characteristic, so to speak. It has been found in all classes of men ; in the heathen, in the philosopher, and in the babe in intellect. This is the seed of God, that can never perish, but must be immortal as He is immortal. The chain of life, then, runs through all creation, binding all together, and into it is breathed the true breath of the Divine, giving to all a new and higher life which is their true " ego," and which shall endure when heaven, and earth, and all manifested being shall have passed away.

RETROSPECTIVE.

When we thus view life as a whole, many of the difficulties as to its mere outward, phenomenal differences are removed, and the problems of sin and suffering are more easily solved.

Think of Life as the pulse of God beating in the body of humanity : think of the Divine breath seeking to infuse and expand the physical : think of it as the soul of force, as the soul of motion, seeking ever to express itself, to become in conscious being what it is in essential spirit.

All circumstances, all influences that seem to be evil or against the best welfare of any human being are only apparently so ; the hidden life seeks for such surroundings as shall aid it to develope, and to grow in the best possible manner. The true metal—first mixed with clay—seeks the acid of suffering, and mixing and fusing with that acid is parted from the earth, and shows itself in its true nature. When we get rid of all idea of a man being punished, condemned, or even injured by his inherited tendencies or by the evil example of others, we shall have some clouds removed from our vision, and shall have confidence in the absolute fairness of his destiny.

"Lord, which did sin, this man, or his

parents, that he was born blind?" "Neither this man, nor his parents; but that the glory of God should be manifested." That is; not that God should be made more worthy of honour by causing a miracle to be performed, but that the glory of God should be made manifest by the man becoming through his blindness and its removal, what he could not have become in any other way.

We do not imply by this that there is no such thing as sin and its consequences; we may, we do hinder and retard our progress by our own folly, but these sins are after all but partial and superficial; we shall soon escape from them and rise into a higher and clearer atmosphere. What we need to do in considering life is to look upon it as a whole. Proceeding forth from God, born of Him, the Divine breath incarnates itself for a time in clay: it rises from the non-sentient to the sentient: to the conscious and the God-conscious until we stand complete, perfect, the I AM!

Man, then, is in no wise the victim of circumstances, he rather is placed in such surroundings as shall aid him in his upward path. The true ego never sins, and cannot, being born of God; he is immaculate, perfect; it is only in the physical and psychical that these dark shadows exist for a time, to give shelter to the tender spirit.

None then can say to his brother, "I have no need of thee;" we are one, and to destroy a part, if that were possible, would be to destroy the whole.

In the early stages of our life we say: "The kingdom of Heaven is at hand"; but when we have advanced a stage farther in true wisdom we say: "The kingdom of Heaven is within us." Let us strive, then, to fight with and overcome these opposing, but helping forces; that in the striving we may become strong, and may be reconciled with, and united to, those very things which seem to be against us: let us struggle to break free from the bondage of our physical

B

nature, when that holds us too firmly, and let our folded wings expand and carry us to the psychical, then again we shall burst that covering and rise to the spiritual.

Briefly to recapitulate then :

There is One—the nameless, the Infinite—

He becomes man, and manifests himself in phenomena.

This manifestation becomes more and more complete, until it may be said to again withdraw from phenomena, and (though still self-conscious) return to the bosom of the Infinite.

Now, dear friends, we have given you, very shortly, some of the articles of our creed, that you may better understand the point of view which we take in our survey of life here and hereafter. This is the faith of many, but certainly not of all : of the differences in faith we will speak more at length when we come to the religions of the Hades and Heavenly States ; this will suffice for the present to bring us 'en rapport' while we talk together.

THE ARTICLE OF DEATH.

" He is not here, he is risen : come see the ' form '
where the Loid lay."

" Behold, I show you a mystery : we shall all be
changed : for this corruptible must put on incorruption,
and this mortal must put on immortality."

The point at which your life joins ours is that
experience, that change which we call death : a
change—really so natural, so simple, so universal—which has yet been more dreaded by
humanity than any suffering which was supposed to come after.

In the truest sense, however, there is no death.

There is no death even to the physical, if by
death we understand destruction or annihilation :
for what happens to the physical is merely dis-
integration : a dissolving of the earthly frame,
that it may be built up again in a new form, while
the true life escapes from its prison.

The psychical does not dwell in the physical
as a man dwells in a house, or as a jewel may lie
in a casket : rather it permeates and infuses the

whole as a perfume inhabits a flower, as a sound fills space, as love fills the heart.

There are, as you have often been told, no violent changes, no forced or hasty developments in nature ; therefore what seems to be violent is not really so ; and those changes which seem to be unconnected with what goes before or after are so only in appearance. Birth and death are only apparently unconnected with the past or the future, and that because to you only the one side is visible. *You* see the death on your side, and *we* see the birth into ours. When an infant dies the psyche has not yet fully manifested itself, is not so closely connected with its phenomenon as it would be later, and it parts from it most easily ; but it comes into this life an immature being, and needs careful nursing and guarding before it attains its true manhood. The most natural death is that of the man or woman in the full possession of his powers, when such powers have been as fully developed as was possible on your plane.

Then, when the bodily faculties begin to decay, the psychical loses its hold on the physical, can no longer manifest itself through the body, and the unused higher powers sleep for a time. But in all cases there is no real break at death, hardly as much as comes to you in sleep ; the man disappears from your sight and appears in ours, like a ship sinking below your horizon, and appearing above the horizon of other lands, without consciously rising or falling to those on her decks. So when your call comes, do not seek to hide in your clay prison, fearing you should be found naked ; but be ready that when the Master calls you may at once go forth—without fear and without regret for the body cast off—and you shall be found clothed in the likeness of God ; for as we have borne the image of the earthly, so also shall we bear the image of the heavenly !

THE PASSING.

" Our birth is but a sleep and a forgetting ;
   The soul that rises with us, our life's star,
   Hath had elsewhere its setting,
   And cometh from afar :
   Not in entire forgetfulness,
   And not in utter nakedness,
   But trailing clouds of glory do we come
   To God, who is our home."

Our birth into this new life differs in almost
every point from our birth into the earthly. We
owe our earthly body to others ; our psychic
body to ourselves. That is, the state of development in which we arrive here depends greatly on
our past life, and we may be said to be born here
as infants, children, or mature beings according
to the past life and the present state of the true
self. Our psychic body is being formed within
the earthly during our earthly life, but the
materials of which it is composed are not earthly,
but are finer, rarer, though still material, and
capable of outward manifestation to the psychic
vision. The clay out of which the Spirit of Life

creates our new bodies is not the old red earth, not the old Adam; but is like unto the resurrection body of the Master; a body which could not see corruption, and which the grave could not hold, though it might be guarded ever so closely.

The psyche, then, when it has quitted the earthly tenement appears immediately and suddenly in this: just as you see a man when he emerges from his house; a moment ago he was invisible to you, now he is completely visible. So it is here; the body, which is the only part of a man visible to your eyes, is the part that is invisible to us and hides him from us. Sometimes he appears for a moment here—shadowy and unreal, more like a vision—then disappears again for a while. This is when the soul is loth to leave the body and lingers near it.

When the time arrives for the psyche to quit the earthly plane, and leave its earthly covering behind it, then the link which unites it to the physical is broken. This link partakes of the two natures, and the only pain and struggle connected with this passing is when the soul is unwilling to loose its hold on the earthly, or fears to do so. Then a moment of unconsciousness supervenes : a time of longer or shorter duration, according to circumstances. The psychical does not generally quit the body immediately, but slowly withdraws itself, and then only the body gradually decays and disintegrates : the lower forms of life escape to re-incarnate themselves in some other form, while there must always be a certain degree of life abiding in each atom, for without it they would have no existence. So the spirit of the animal goeth downward, remaining in the earthly sphere, and the spirit of the man goeth upward, entering into the higher life.

We now have the man, divested of his lower form, ready to enter into the intermediate state. And with what body does he come? With one that closely resembles the earthly one—very closely indeed at first—but with powers infolded within it that far transcend the old ones, though those powers are yet more or less dormant. The man is still far from being pure spirit ; he bears a form like the Master's, a form which is in four dimensions,* and which cannot be seen by ordinary earthly vision. The old body is the matrix in which the new man is formed, and from which, by the pangs of death he is parted, to enter into his second life. Now how does he appear on our side ? Our eyes do not see the physical, that you always must bear in mind. What we see of the earthly is only the soul-image reflected in some medium. It is therefore after this uncovering that the new-born appears within the scope of our vision. He awakes, and finds himself in a state that seems to him at first but the same to which he has been accustomed ; he continues—as he thinks—his old life, until the fact gradually dawns upon him that the great change has taken

*See Appendix on " Dimensions."

place, and that he has passed from death unto
life.

The Psychic Sleep.

"So He giveth His beloved sleep."

And now the psyche sleeps for a while, for a
few hours, days or years, according to your ideas
of time.   This " sleep," as we implied, is not that
of unconsciousness ; we call it so because it
resembles your sleep greatly in this ; that the
sleeper is unconscious of his actual surroundings,
while he moves and lives in fancy in other times
and states.   The length and character of this
sleep depend entirely on the state of the man
when he passed over : depend that is on what he
was in his earthly life.   (Why such differences
exist will be spoken of more fully when we come
to deal with the psychic character.) What are the
soul experiences during this sleep, and what are the
appearance and actions of the sleeper as viewed
by us ? His experiences are as manifold, as
different the one from the other as he differs in

himself; for no two souls are alike, and no two can have exactly the same experience : diversity in unity is the law of our nature. To some there is a re-living of the past life, a taking up of broken threads, and a weaving of them together in a more finished manner : perhaps the failings are now first seen in their true light ; the clouds of self-deception caused by self-love, wilful transgression, etc., fade away, and a soul can look back upon his past life with a clear and true vision, and when the soul thus truly sees and knows good and evil, it can but choose the good and refuse the evil. Others imagine that they continue their life, and starting with all the old habits and prejudices they gradually drop the evil, and are strengthened in the good.

Paul said, "We shall not all sleep ; " and there is much truth in this ; for to some it is of such a brief duration that it may be more truly called a change, in a moment, in the twinkling of an eye.

We now ask—What is the aspect in which we

regard these sleepers, and what is their connec-
tion with us? We look upon them much as you
do on very young children : we care for them and
guard them in much the same way. There is no
sense of unfitness in their ignorance, and we can
feel neither surprise when they awake quickly,
nor impatience if the state is prolonged ; for it is
simply that their new powers are not yet adjusted
to their new environment. They are not pur-
posely deceived as to their state, but even if we
should wish to tell them where and what they
were, it would be as incomprehensible to them as
deep philosophy to a young child. Then they
need food : food which is the counterpart of
yours, and they need employment in such ways
as most resemble the old duties. In these and
other ways, their past life is gently and gradually
withdrawn from the prominent place in their
mental horizon which it formerly filled, and the
new rises, like a new day, upon their clearer
vision. In different ways the call comes to them

to awake out of their sleep, and arise from the earthly, and walk in newness of life.

Will you always bear in mind that when we say—such and such things occur, or in this way the soul developes—we do not lay down any hard and fast law as to manner or sequence of development; rather we give you what is most general in our circle and in our experience. But as one flower unfolds and expands differently from another, so is it with the soul.

The following history was received at an earlier period, and has been inserted here at the request of the writer of the book, that it may serve as an illustration of the Psyche's experience after "the passing":—

When I first awoke, I thought I was a girl again, and that the latter part of my earthly life had not yet been lived, but that my memory of it was only a dream, an imagination. Then, in a kind of vision (but I thought it a reality), I continued my life from my girlhood, and in the hour

of great temptation—remembering my supposed
dream—I withstood. Again the scene changed,
and again I took up the thread of life at the
same part as before. This time I yielded to
temptation, but instead of keeping the birth of
my child secret, I brought him up as my own,
and trained him as well as I could. One day
I awoke to the consciousness that I had died,
and oh! the rest and peace were great. After
some time I met my sister, and began my real
life here, but it has been much easier for that
vision-life that I had at the first.

I will try to make our life a little clearer to
you. In your world the will can only produce
things when joined to power of some sort. With
us the will can and does create our surroundings.
I mean by this that what we earnestly desire is
in a moment evolved and completed, provided
that our will is in harmony with the over-will of
the Divine. If I will a home, that home stands
immediately complete before me. When I met

my sister it had been her wish to live alone.
Her life, therefore, was not so complete as it
might have been. For my sake, however, she
gave up her wanderings, and at a wish our home
was ready, and we have dwelt there ever since.
Our life and our home closely resemble the lives
and homes of earth, and this resemblance they
will keep for some time ; but as progress is the
law for everyone, and as in their turn these new
bodies of ours will seem gross and earthly, so we
must cast them off and pass into higher spheres.
But even here we are far in advance of you. If
we really desire to know anything we know it
without mistake. If we really desire to do anything for another, we see clearly what to do, and
can do it. Only the will is needed, then there is
no limit unless it would be hurtful to anyone.
If we need what we had not got for anyone,
a wish would produce it, just as the Master could
produce the loaves when he had a strong feeling
of pity for the poor hungry souls around him.

Our life is portioned out into what answers
to your mental and manual employments. We
have the outward, and we have the inward ; we
work and we play ; we talk and we think ; we
meet those that we love, and are parted from
them again ; we make new friends, and we love
more and more the old ones. There is no
mistake and no failure, as I say, except our own
will fails. In that case sorrow and repentance
have to follow : we try again, and walk in a plain
path in which there is no need to stumble.
Since I have been in this new home I have known
what peace, love, and joy really are : all three
unbroken, and increasing every day. I am
not permitted to see or know much of the two
whose influence over my earthly life was so great,
but I am perfectly content to have it so. Neither
have I yet gone into that higher sphere ; there is
some good reason for delay.

THE SOUL'S AWAKENING.

With illustrations of different types.

I.—DIVES.

" The poor man died, and was carried by the angels into
Abraham's bosom.
The rich man died and was buried : and in hell he lifted
up his eyes, being in torment."

The sleeper now awakens : that is he becomes
truly conscious of his surroundings: he knows both
what he is and what he has been, and his true
psychic life begins. He enters into that state
which may be said to be the immediate result of
his earthly life ; that state which has been spoken
of as one of punishment and reward ; words that
were true enough in their original meaning, but
which have been so distorted by man's low ideas
that they are more misleading than true. The man
now reaps what he has sown, he enters into the
possession of the treasure that he has laid up, or
he finds himself naked and poor. The poor in
spirit become rich, while the rich unto themselves

alone are so poor that they cannot even get water to quench their thirst. In what manner do they suffer? In the inimitable story told by the Master from which we have quoted, physical terms are used to describe the psychical, and this as a matter of necessity.

How is it physically when you suffer cold or heat? It is that your body is out of harmony with its surroundings. When you feel cold it is because the temperature of your body is higher than the air around you, and when you suffer from heat it is because your temperature is lower. When the affections of the soul are cold and almost dead, then it cannot bear the heat of the heavenly atmosphere—full of love and pity— which surrounds it; it is a hell of fire. The rich man asked for water, and apparently he did not obtain it; but the moment he began to care for, and remember others, at that moment his thirst began to be quenched, and the intolerable torment to diminish. " Between us is a great gulf fixed."

This gulf is not one of place, nor of time : it is no artificial barrier, but simply the great gulf which separates, for a time, those who are not one in spirit. Even on your earth there may be two most closely united outwardly, but within, heaven and hell are not so far apart as their spirits. So we do not in our state separate the evil from the good, the tares from the wheat ; but both grow together until the day when the evil has died in the furnace of suffering, and the wheat is ready to be gathered into the heavenly garner.

II.—LAZARUS.

Lazarus, the poor man, is a good type of another large class. There are many who let themselves be borne along by the force of circumstances, without any struggle to make nature subservient to them. Such people are generally poor, and let themselves be oppressed by the tyrant; they simply suffer when they might find a remedy for their complaint, and their faculties, being not misused, but unused, lie dormant, and so are feeble when they come over. Such, indeed, need to be carried by angels into Abraham's bosom, where the mere absence of physical discomfort produces a sense of happiness for a time, and the great gulf keeps them from all activity until they have grown a little stronger.

So they are comforted, and when strong enough, they too will take their share in the furnace that purifies. No impatience, however, nor contempt, is felt by the " angels " for such a class ; for in our wider views of life we see, that by many paths all will be led in time to the heavenly city.

III.—THE CARNAL MAN.

The next class includes those whose spirits are so earth-bound that they seem unable to tear themselves away from their former surroundings. Those whose passions have been strong on earth, and strong for earth alone, finding little or nothing in their new life which is sympathetic to them, return in spirit to the world they have quitted, and live over and over again the past. From this class most of the appearances, the *revenants* are drawn ; for anxious to renew, however faintly, their old impressions, they draw to themselves a physical covering, a body, which as a medium they can use to see, and hear, and know the old life. This, however, they succeed in doing but very partially, for the link between the psychical and the physical is not truly re-united, and the sensations are but dim and shadowy. It is such as these that have been sometimes helped by counsel from those on your side.

IV.—THE IDOLATER.

The next class includes those whose lives— outwardly correct—have yet been wanting in the true spirit of love, so that they have been really dead while they seemed to live. With a strong sense of their own righteousness and with low thoughts of others, these Pharisees, these idolaters, of whatever sect or religion they may have been, have their nature completely engrossed with the one idea of their own goodness or sufficiency. When they look back upon their past life, this constant habit of the mind prevents them from acknowledging any failure, any fault, and in a self-justifying spirit they see nothing but their own reflection in the pool of memory, and so for a long time they remain in the valley, where the Sun of Life cannot warm them with its rays. Such are helped to true repentance, and hatred of their former state by seeing the noble self-sacrificing lives of those who are most truly wise ; and it is by such examples, and willing self devotion that these troubled ones are comforted.

THE POOL OF MEMORY.

A letter from one who thus helped these earth-bound souls.

" TO A FRIEND.—It has been shown me that now soon I must—nay I may—die on the cross of self-sacrifice to this state. It has seemed a blissful one to me, a heavenly Jerusalem, and in my ignorance I should not even have sought a better. Between my death to the old and resurrection to the new I am permitted to visit the souls ' in prison,' and by the power I have obtained set free *one* soul that has been bound perhaps forty years. Is there one that you would wish to commend to me ? Yes, I see there is one, who without help must remain on the edge of the pool, and her I will help. When I am lifted up, I will draw her up also from the grave to the open day. I have no need to explain to you, dear friends, that the metaphors I use are very faulty. The Pool into which these poor lost souls are ever gazing reflects only the broken images of their past lives ; they see them in all their deformity and poverty ; over and over again do they live through the past, conscious of their defects, yet unable to remedy them until they are willing to acknowledge that they have been wrong. On the other hand there is no food for self-love in their surroundings ; no one on whom to expend the evil force of their nature, no room for self in any way. But this is really a blessing, for the evil is thus starved out of them, and into their empty hearts can then come the power of love which they see has been ever around them although they knew it not. This knowledge penetrates the hardest heart, and with a cry for help and pardon a new soul is born within them, and the second death is past. The purple shadows of night are lost in the golden glories of a new day, and a new earth and a new heaven rise to their view. But oh ! the sadness it is to see some not yet ready for this awakening breath of the Divine spirit,—to have to leave them behind for many days, or even years. How hard is the human will before it responds to the magnetic touch of Love—oh! how hard!"

V.—THE CHILD.

Again, we have very many dear, simple souls who come over after a life of loving devotion to the highest duty they know of; such souls need but little discipline; and a simple life of simple duties, a home where they can shelter and help the " sleepers," a life like a glorified earthly one: such is their gentle and gradual development, almost unmarked in its changes day by day, yet surely rising and expanding.

The mother's story which you have previously received will best illustrate this childlike spirit.

A MOTHER'S EXPERIENCE.
Addressed to her grown-up daughters.

" MY DEAR DAUGHTERS.—I know you all thought and hoped that your mother when she

died went to heaven, but since then you have
learned more of the life after death, and you will not
be surprised when I tell you that I have not yet
even seen the gates of heaven. Yet I am really
happy, yes very happy, as I could not have been
if this place had been what I expected. When I
first woke up it seemed like earth, only I thought
I had crossed somehow to a new country. I
expected your father to join me by-and-by,
and bring the children with him (for I thought
you were still all little ones). The air was so
sweet and the people all so kind, and I said:
' I must not be idle till the others come,' so
I got work to do, clothes to make, it seemed to
be. Then one day I remembered suddenly about
Sunday, and I asked where the church was. The
person I asked smiled and said softly, ' this is the
church : this world is the temple not made with
hands where we worship the Father.' As she
spoke, a shock went through me, and I heard
hundreds of voices saying, ' Praise Him, praise

the everlasting King.' Then in a moment it was shown me that I had died, and these were spirits round me ; yet I had no fear at all, only a great wonder. I knelt down and said the Lord's Prayer, for that was all that I could remember just then. Although I knew, as I have said, that I had died, yet it seemed impossible to believe it, for everything was so different from what I had been taught to expect. I said to my friend : ' How is it that my body is here ; I thought it would be left in the grave.' She said, ' yes, that body is in the grave ; the one you have is a new one, and very different from the old. Did you not think you were young ? Yet when you died you were old, and your body nearly worn out.' Then I remembered the latter part of my life, and things seemed stranger than ever. ' But I thought we should be like angels, and have wings,' I said. ' You have not got wings exactly,' she replied, ' but if you want to pass quickly from this place to any other, you can : Take my hand

and try.' We seemed to fly, and in a moment
we were in a different place; I saw your
father leading an old man by the hand and talk-
ing to him, but my tongue was tied, and I could
not speak to him. Then we flew back again, and
I was left to myself to try and settle my thoughts,
which were so confused. I said to myself that
surely in heaven,—for that was where I thought
myself,—in heaven they all sing psalms, and I
cannot sing a note; and they all wear white robes
and have harps in their hands; yet I saw none of
these things, nor any throne.

Then a voice seemed to whisper in my ear,
and it said : 'The white robe is what you have
been working at here ; it is ready now :' the psalm
was the Our Father, which sounded like music in
my ear, and the throne, my throne is in your
heart. And then, my dear children, I first began
really to understand, and a deep peace came over
me. But I could never tell you half how I found
out one thing after another ; what new powers I

had, and how wonderful everything seemed ; but I kept saying, 'Speak, Lord, for thy servant heareth;' while the voice continually whispered to me and taught me to understand. After that time I did not do much work, for I was busy learning : I was told that as my life had been filled with outward work, work done mostly with my hands, I was now to be taught to think : and because my life had been all taken up with my family, I was to live for a time with strangers : not that I had been wrong so much as one-sided, only half of me having grown. Now the other half is being made to grow, and every day I learn about the mysteries of God, and of our own life, which are just as wonderful. Perhaps you think that my life is too much like an earthly one, but it is not ; only I cannot explain to you the things that are quite different. It seems to me as if, on earth, people were like dead things compared to what we are here. One thing in the life here might seem strange to you : it is that the best

and highest live almost constantly with those
who are troubled and suffering—for there is
suffering here—awful anguish sometimes, but I
need not tell you about that, as it would do no
good. I am not called upon to take part in this
service yet, but when I am fit, I shall be willing.
Your father has both suffered and been allowed
to help others : his life is all busy, while mine is
quiet, or only busy in learning. I have not seen
any angel, or any one but human beings yet.
We have worship, and the music and words are
our own : each time they spring up in our hearts
like a fountain, yet it all goes well together. I
am never tired now, nor get weary of what I
have to do : I do not know if the time is long or
short, but I suppose I have been here a few years
now. It was given to me to come and tell you a
few things, and when others have written I have
always known what they have told you. Do you
wonder what there is here to make me so happy ?
We are happy because we know God loves us,

and we love Him back, and that makes us blessed. He teaches me by the voice of His dear Son, and He will teach you all, that when you join me here, you will not have so much to learn, or so long to wait before getting your new soul and going up higher. I should like to look after some of the little motherless children who come here, but I am not chosen to do that work.

Dear children, be sure to see that your minds and souls grow as well as your hearts and bodies. Every loving, true word, and every simple, righteous action is treasure laid up in heaven. Live so that when you come over you may not be poor and ashamed, but may be strong and able to help others. If you are lifted up in spirit while still living on the earth, you will draw up others as our Lord did. Every thought is a seed, and every word a root from which must spring up a harvest either of wheat or tares. Try to sow good seed that you may have sheaves of ripe corn to lay at the Master's feet by-and-by.

VI.—THE TRUE MAN.

The next class includes those who have lived true, full lives upon earth : whose psychic powers, while still incarnated in flesh, were being highly developed ; those of whom the world was not worthy, the flower of humanity and its fruit. Not faultless, of course, nor yet by any means perfectly developed in all directions, yet having advanced so far that they are fit for other experiences than those we have already indicated. After a short sleep they awake strong, and ready for the service of their fellows. At first they generally use most easily those faculties which have been strongest on earth. The philosopher imparts wisdom to the simple ; the poet sings to the sad sweet songs of love ; the man of business directs and strengthens the weak. It is from this class that the saviours of the psychic sphere are drawn ; with full hearts and wise heads they are ready to work, to suffer, to sacrifice themselves in any way, if in the slightest degree they can help their brethren to see the beauty of true, unselfish lives. You, dear friends, know one grand type of this class, and there are many like him.

VII.—THE PERFECT MAN.

Lastly : The highest and the most perfect that we have ever known or dreamed of is the Master. In other ages, and in other climes there may have been one or two that nearly reached the height of His perfection ; but to us there is only one. Having passed through the earthly life without failure in any moral duty, and with singleness of heart from first to last, always reaching after the highest ideals ; in him the perfect, the ideal manhood was manifest. After a brief psychic sleep, he rises in the full possession of his new powers, and uncontrolled in the least by mere circumstance, he bends all things to the accomplishment of his high and loving purpose, and sets himself to raise his brethren to the level of his own perfect life.

These few illustrations will be enough to give you an idea of the " soul's awakening," and of its new life in the earlier stages. The soul's expansion will come later. Do not interpret our words too literally, or think these classes are marked off too sharply ; no, they blend into each other as do the good and evil on earth.

CONDITIONS OF LIFE IN THE PSYCHIC WORLD. TIME, SPACE, VISION, HEARING, &c.

> " Time's wheel runs back or stops ;
> Potter and clay endure."

What has already been given you on dimensions will save us much repetition, and we need therefore add but a few words on each division.*

You must remember that we are still in an intermediate and transitory state : that even here we are not what we shall be ; that we are still limited in various ways and degrees.

Time.—" One day is with the Lord as a thousand years, and a thousand years as one day."

In the earthly life the limitations of time are greatest in the physical, less in the mental, still less in the spiritual side of your nature. In strict reality the moments roll on, one by one, each filled by the same amount of motion and active force in the invisible atoms making up the molecules of which phenomena consist : but in

---

See Appendix.

the mental life the thoughts, the memory can live through a year in a few moments, or mental anguish may draw out a moment into an hour. The spirit seems almost beyond these laws of time—and love, truth, justice, pity are not of time, but beyond it. In our life we enter into the second of these states which becomes our lower one, we are not beyond the influence of time, but we are less strictly bound by it.

Two may pass over from your world on the same day, and may awake from the psychic sleep together ; yet one may have had almost a lifetime's experience, and the other may have been only conscious of the passing of a few days. No time with us seems long when we live as we ought,—nor on the contrary does any work lack completion for want of time for its accomplishment. " And the angel being caused to fly swiftly came unto Daniel at the time of evening sacrifice." This well represents our state : are we called to any work it can be done ; but should the duty not be laid upon us, then the opportunity would not be given. These bonds of time do not fall from us immediately, but are rather loosened, and with other earthly limitations they fall from us one by one.

Space.—To what has already been said in dimensions, we need only add that we go wheresoever a true need or worthy desire may lead us : we are with those who are one with us in spirit, and though many in all stages of experience and character may be said to be literally in the same place, yet they are not truly with us unless we can help them in some way .

"When thou wast under the fig tree, I saw thee."

Hearing, Vision, Etc.—This was no vain boast, nor yet a miracle : but the Master, as being more perfect than most, and having His psychic powers already far developed, could see all that He truly needed to see ; both of outward things and of inner secrets of the heart. We, too, read each other's hearts when the wish or need to do so

arises ; our powers in all these matters, you will
understand, not being perfunctory, can only be
exercised where and in what degree the soul
truly requires. So also with speech ; my words
or audible thoughts can only reach another if
those words will help or interest him, or express
my love to him : no others can be interpreted
by any ; they would only fall upon his ear like
the sighing of the breeze, or the wordless sounds
with which your world is so full. The old grave
clothes, you see, are being cast off, folded away, and
in white and shining garments the new man pre-
pares to rise to another still better and fairer state.

THE PSYCHE.

" The future I may face
Now I have proved the Past."
" Take this child and nurse it for me, and I will give thee
thy wages."
" And he brought him to an inn, and took out two pence,
and gave them to the host, and said : Take care of
him, and whatsoever thou spendest more, when I
come again I will repay thee."

Before proceeding to describe the life here
more fully, it may be well to say something on

man himself, and the reason why his surroundings and destiny are so varied.

Why hast thou made us to differ? Why do some suffer anguish of body and misery of soul, while others have no cross in their lot? Is this not a common cry? But it arises simply from our short-sightedness : from the small, the very small portion of our life which alone is open to our gaze, but which self-love and self-pity magnify until it fills not only our earthly, but also our heavenly horizon. We must take large views of life if we would understand it at all clearly. We must think of man as passing from eternity to eternity across the narrow bridge of time : as coming from the invisible All-Father,—made manifest for a brief day, and then returning to the bosom of the Infinite. Incarnated first in the lowest phenomena ; rising through the dead stone, the living plant, the animal, to the man— then disappearing to the eye of sense and living purely in the spirit.

Now as each human ego differs in manifested life from every other, it needs a different experience, and to each is given the material (so to speak) from which it can derive the food best suited to its special needs. Some can only grow when their roots have struck deep in the black earth of sin ; others require the knife of the pruner freely applied to them ; while to others only sunshine and the dews of heaven seem necessary : to each the best and most suitable surroundings are given.

As souls pass over in all stages of their development, their life nas to be very varied. On the other hand, the difference between one man's destiny and another's is not so great as it appears, especially if you could take the sum of their experiences. If your eyes could see the heart as well as the life, and understand the deepest springs of motive, and know fully all the powers of inherited evil, of susceptibility to influence, then many of the " good and evil "

would stand on a greater equality in your esti-
mation. Those crimes which shock you most
are often small things in our eyes; for much
belongs to the physical and will drop off from
the psyche at death, as the outer covering of the
leaf-bud when it comes forth in its perfection. It
is that spirit which says to its brother: "Am I
thy keeper?" which is most hurtful to the soul:
but whatever it may be, sin or suffering, good or
evil, joy or misery, all shall have the appointed
end in nursing the infant soul.

I used these well-known words as a heading,
because it seems as if the Father said to Nature,
with reference to the soul: "Take this child and
nurse it for me," and the physical proves the best
nurse that we can have. Then when we have
grown to manhood we are passed on to the care
of those in the psychic world, and they watch
over us and help us until the wounds are all
healed, and our strength restored, so that we can
begin a new and worthy life.

We must now speak of the state of the man
when he has cast off his physical body. That
state depends, as we have said, on the degree
of development that he has already attained.
He is now psyche and spirit. His psychical body
is the image of his physical one ; not inferior, but
superior ; the blossom of the seed, yet still the
blossom of that particular seed, and not of another.
Now he has to go through varied experiences until
instead of the psychic dominating the spirit, or the
two being evenly balanced, the spirit becomes
entirely the master, and the psyche the servant.
Then the man is ready to depart into the heavenlies,
having finished the task that was given him to do.

We say that at first the psyche is generally
supreme. The life then is much like the earthly
one ; food is necessary, they live in houses, they
work, they rest, but yet with a difference. You
need food and rest at stated intervals, but here
they are only needed when the spirit is not strong
enough to supply the body. We hear of some

fasting in your world, and when the will is strong enough to control the body it can be done. With us it is always so ; that is, the body only needs refreshment when the faith fails, or is too weak. Gradually and with many failures and retrogressive steps the soul and spirit become first equal, then the spirit is master, and finally the psychic envelope is burst, and the spirit rises free and untrammelled. The pneuma, when it is strong enough, goes to its home for a time, and then returns. This it may do often and over a long period, before it finally leaves. Generally, however, we believe, about half a century is the limit of its stay in the Hades or intermediate state.

> And then the Ship
> Complete at last,—loosed from its earthly bonds,
> Glides from its birthplace to the sea:
> Which yielding, yet supporting, bears it on,
> Out from the land-locked harbour to the deep.
> Cumbrous before, it lay upon the stocks
> Like some dead thing, neither of earth nor air:
> But now it lives, and guided by the winds
> Leaves earth behind it, and sails onward to the sun.

THE NEW LIFE.

And now, dear friends, that we have told you of the new surroundings in which the soul finds himself and something of the new powers which he possesses, we must next tell you more definitely of what he does, and how his life is lived.

On earth you have some kinds of labour that are almost purely physical, requiring little, if any, mental capacity, and no spiritual insight. Say a man spends his days in sticking pins into paper by the help of machinery; or breaks stones at the road-side. These occupations are almost entirely physical,—though I would not deny that mind and soul could be exercised even in such tasks—but they will do for an example. How much difference is there between such labour and that of an engineer planning and carrying out the making of some mighty tunnel, or bridge. The difference is still more marked between your works and ours, and yet the resemblance is great also. With us the purely physical is past, and we have as little of that as the stonebreaker has of the mental; but the old habits remain, and the new-born soul finds it as difficult to exercise his new powers as the untaught boy to use the artist's brush. Only by degrees, quicker or slower according to past life and present powers, is he able to work and act with the soul, instead of with the body. Instead of the hands building our houses, our trained will builds them. Your friends told you that if they needed anything and willed it, it stood complete before them. That was true, but such power is not attained all at once; it is gradual. The desires, the reason, the affections must be in harmony, and then we can do our work. Imagine yourself then here on our side with your first psychic sleep over, the early stages of repentance and faith past, and you now ready to be a citizen of the new Jerusalem.

Hitherto your wants have been supplied by others; now—let us say—you wish to make for yourself a home where you may wait for the loved ones to join you. If this is best for you, you can then think out what you want. Perhaps your thought will be broken, incomplete; and what rises before your pyschic vision may be faulty and incongruous. Well, you will then dissolve it again into the unseen but real "elements" (to use an old word), and try again.

You have no money, of course, to buy from others what they may possess, but if you need anything it will be gladly and freely given you; only in return you must give something—gratitude, sympathy, or some other soul gift.

Having got rid of so much that is physical, we have lost two things that make much of the discomfort of your world—I mean dirt and decay. In your world the repulsive form which decay takes is owing to the very slow way in which dead or dying matter disintegrates; but with us all change of that sort is more rapid : the life escapes easily from its psychic form to re-appear in others ; therefore we have dissolution, but not decay.

At first you will need food, more or less
frequently ; but as time goes on this food will be
less and less necessary, and the senses will be
satisfied in other ways : the perfume, the beauty
of the fruit will be sufficient. This food has a
close relationship to yours, but is strictly vegetable and simple ; that is you eat the seed or the
fruit as it grows, without changing or combining :
such fruit you can cultivate for yourself, or receive
from others if you should be engaged in other
forms of work.

The clothing, or outward form in which you
appear to others, grows on you, so to speak, and
is the outcome of your true state ; more or less
affording pleasure to those who see you, as it
is more or less harmonious, and the reflex of a
true and earnest spirit.

Sleep, I think we have already said, falls
upon you as the mind needs rest. If your new
powers are overtaxed, then a period of rest—
longer or shorter —comes upon you ; for the

psyche can tire as the mind or brain tires upon
earth.

Then as to occupation : the soul naturally
turns to some occupation most closely resembling
that to which it has been accustomed, but it is not
permitted to remain in it too long. The nature
all round has to be cultivated ; and as no wisdom is gained apart from learning and experience, so it is necessary that the man who in his
past life has yielded to others and been ruled by
them, should learn to advise, control, and help :
that the man who has lived apart from nature in
the world of books, or of the imagination, should
now sow, reap, and understand the beauty of the
new earth into which he has passed. Or again,
the one who has lived entirely in the outward,
must learn to withdraw into himself, or to study
the wisdom of those who have climbed the steeps
of knowledge before him.

The great, the unspeakable difference, however, between the old and the new is the absolute

freedom of the new. No one can either hinder or compel another in any way, and no one wishes to do so.

Faults there are and imperfections, mistakes and weaknesses, but a great spirit of love and unselfishness is the very atmosphere of the place, and none would cast the smallest stumbling-block in the way of his brother.

Now does this absence of the physical seem to make our world shadowy and unreal to you ? If so, get rid of the idea immediately. Does a man who has walked with crutches feel that he has exchanged the real for the visionary when— healed and strong— he casts them away and exercises his own true powers? No, indeed, and neither do we ; we feel that iron fetters have dropped from us, and that now for the first time we know what real living means : life so full, so deep and satisfying that the past is only as the shadow of a dream that passes away in the light of a new day.

Then as to language : we do not speak another
language from those of earth · that is not another
added to, yet different from those, as Hebrew is
another language differing from English.   Our
language is a universal, primeval instinct (so to
speak).   We impress our thoughts on one another
by and through the will power, and our language
is limited, not by words, but by our own power
of feeling and by the hearer's power of sympathy.
This language is only the perfection of those
powers which are in every human being, though
nearly dormant, and which have been weakened
through long ages of disuse, and by a more
artificial speech.   There are many things, such
as the universal needs of the body, or the simple
passions which can be expressed and understood
by all independently of mere words.   Joy, fear,
grief, hunger, love, need no words, and can be
expressed by and through the eye.   Even the
outward is not always necessary, for one can
influence and control the thoughts and feelings of

others even without the bodily presence. So we impress our thoughts on others here, first in a weak and broken manner, like a child learning to talk, and then more and more fully as our soul expands ; also as we gain more experience in this life our vocabulary increases. Then with regard to others' powers of understanding us : this, too, does not depend on any artificial acquirement of mere words, nor yet on what would answer to the power of the intellect, for a philosopher does not necessarily understand me better than a child, but the power of comprehension equals the power of sympathy ; and by sympathy, I mean the capability of feeling as the speaker does, were you in his circumstances.

Again, this is only the natural human method enlarged and rectified, for the knowledge of words alone does not enable you to enter into the heart and mind of the speaker. Linnæus kneeling before the glorious works of God, with hands folded and eyes upraised in worship, would be to some a true child of nature, acting in the most natural and simple manner : to another he might be only a fool or a drunkard. "These men are filled with new wine," some say, while others— "we do hear in our own language the wonderful works of God ;" and yet again to others it might be merely "a pleasant sound as of one playing on an instrument."

Still we are not in our world without that joy which arises from musical sounds ; only such sounds are not caused by vibrations of the atmosphere, but by vibrations of the soul-currents, which are heard inwardly by those whose souls are attuned to the same key.

You will say, perhaps, why should I need a house now I have got rid of my more material body ? It is true that a house is not essential, any more than it is essential on earth ; but the instincts underneath, the desire for shelter, safety, privacy—the closer companionship of some than of all ; these feelings still exist, especially at first.

Until the psyche becomes perfect in strength and beauty there will be at times a sense of discord with his surroundings, which will be as a cold or wet day to your bodies. Then again, the timid or suffering soul may, and does often shrink from the presence and inspection of those to whom it feels as you do to strangers who may be unsympathetic to you. All such feelings, or many of them remain when the soul is parted from the body, and it is some time before they modify or disappear. Because there is no real cause for such fear is no reason why it should not exist ; for the man has not changed in any essential point, and will only pass from the lower to the higher by slow and patient striving. After a time we find that there is no need for us to shrink from any ; we learn that the power to read another's thoughts, or to enter into his feelings, depends first on the will of the person observed, and secondly on the sympathetic insight we have spoken of in the observer. Therefore, I am an impenetrable enigma to all unless I wish to unfold myself to them; and even if the wish first exists in me, there must be the response in them. There may be many here, a world within a world, of whom I have no knowledge, simply because I do not hold the key of sympathy which would unlock their gates.

In your world you are at once eternally separated from every other being and yet open to the cold, curious gaze of the crowd. With us we can have the deepest and truest union, and we can also be truly and really withdrawn if we wish.

Now with regard to such possessions as houses, food, land, books. I know it has often been said on your side that here there can be no such things as possessions; that there is nothing but the glorified spirit: that all is intangible, invisible, immortal. This is a mistake which arises partly from confusing our intermediate state with a more advanced one, though even then it would not be absolutely true. No, we have possessions;

things outside of ourselves that can take shape, be, and dissolve again : houses and lands and goods that no moth nor rust can corrupt, nor thieves break through to steal, but yet which, as you have been told, if not rightly used will vanish away. The true and inner law of possession is well understood by you. You know well what it means by the meek inheriting the earth, and that the mere fact of a thing legally or physically belonging to you does not make it truly yours; this is too clear to need illustrating. This inner law is more binding, if possible, here than with you : I can have nothing unless I need it for myself or for another, and I must use it, or it will leave me, as unused mental powers would leave you, vanishing away as though they had not been. We have the outward as well as the inward ; but they are always intimately related : the strength that is not used in highest service vanishes away, and the outward beauty which typifies that strength vanishes likewise.

In trying to describe different phases of our life to you, we must be careful not to lay too much stress on any one phase, and you must guard against letting any one view occupy too large a part of your mental horizon. Life here is so full and so varied, that it is impossible to give you more than a few hints as to its character. We ourselves only know in part, and can only understand the lives of others as we pass through somewhat of their experience.

There is one important *raison d'être* for those possessions of which we have spoken, and that is that we may use them in guarding and teaching the suffering and the ignorant. It has been thought wiser to say but little about the suffering that is endured here by many, nay by all in degree and at times; but we must not overlook it altogether. The gulf that lies between Paradise and hell is not one of physical distance,—no such barrier as that exists.—No, the two may lie closer together than two who are living in the same

house; as close as grief and joy sometimes lie in
ie same heart, Wherever suffering is needed—
riot as a punishment for past misdeeds, but as fire
to burn away the dross,—there it will be found.
Naturally this pain comes generally when we first
pass over, and then when the anguish of the soul
is great, much may be done to teach and support
it by those who have already emerged from the
furnace.

In the homes of all the "saints" may be
found such sufferers ; tenderly watched over,
helped and guarded while the hard lessons are
being learnt. Such learners have cast off but
few of the old instincts, and need to be fed and
protected until they learn to exercise those new
powers which can provide them with all they
need as simply as a flower grows.

In speaking of occupations and of the need
for growth in an all-round way, I may have
given the impression that after all the higher
life is but a selfish one ; an entire absorption

into care for one's own improvement : but this is not so. Combined with it there is always the care of those less advanced ; those who may have grown more than we have in some ways, but less in at least one direction, so that we can say : "This is the way ; walk ye in it." Remember, also, that we are only describing an intermediate state, and that our life, however full, is necessarily incomplete, and still far from that divine ideal which lies ever before our vision.

SCHOOLS.

One marked feature of the life here is that system of united work or study which we have called the "Schools." I speak of myself as belonging to the School of Giotto ; and there are the Schools of Paul, of Zoroaster, of Howard, etc. At least these names would best represent our idea to you. They come about in this way : when the man begins to look round him, and ask himself to what use he had best put his new powers, he begins to think of those things of which he was most ignorant when on earth ; he is then drawn by a law of natural attraction to some who are pursuing the same course, and he finds among them those who have acquired knowledge that has been handed down from the long past, or who are learning by practical life to make such knowledge their own.

Our School, for instance, was in past ages begun by a few who had been drawn to Giotto when he came over. Led and taught by him, they laid up a store of knowledge which should be for others like the stream of health pouring into the veins when one goes from impure to purer air. As there are always some who are studying the beautiful, so there are always students in our university. Of course I have never seen Giotto, he has long ago passed over ; but it is the spirit and power of Giotto which, like the prophet's mantle, rests upon this place.

Again, there are some, who for many reasons do not find a home, a domestic life, congenial to them; yet such need not live solitary; that would be in most cases hurtful. In place of a home they seek the companionship of those who are walking in a similar path, and for months or years they live and work together.

I, myself, had given little thought on earth to beauty; had thought the study of it only an excuse for an idle or inexact order of mind. I had, when I passed over, a great wish to make up for this neglect. Being drawn to these friends, I said: "Teach me what beauty is; let me learn what are its lines and curves; show me how to produce its forms so as to give satisfaction to myself and pleasure to others." There was much narrowness and self-conceit in this request. I thought "Now I shall know the true canon of beauty, and surely I shall appreciate it so well that I shall be an apt scholar." One of our leaders impressed on me a look of divine com-

passion : " We will teach you," he said, " or rather
you shall teach yourself.   Go out from this home
away yonder in the distance ; live there alone,
and depend on the exertions of your will-power
to produce food and shelter for yourself." I went,
of course, knowing there was some good reason
for his command.   I found what seemed a deso-
late barren spot.   I sowed and reaped ; removed
obstructions ; studied nature, and then after a
long time felt myself incited to return.   " Now
go," said my guide, "to yonder city ; live there."
I found in the part to which I seemed drawn a
home full of suffering and deformity—or at least
incompleteness of nature,—but love was there, and
in the midst of their anguish each tried to give a
cup of cold water to the other.   When I returned
again, my friend said : " Beauty is not a matter
of angles and curves ; it is not an abstract idea.
It comes only through the struggle of the lower
with the higher, or rather it is in the higher and
can best be seen when that is breaking through

the lower. You brought beauty out of the earth,
and you saw love bringing beauty out of pain ;
you have learnt much ; now abide here for a time
and help others ; then you shall go to fresh fields
later on."

When we speak of "going and coming," you
will remember our definitions of time and space,
and will understand that like yourselves we cannot be in two places at the same time. Yet our
power of passing to and fro is greatly increased,
as is also the amount of thought and work which
can be compressed into a short space of time.

My next change was to what I have called
the School of Howard ; for I felt drawn to take
some active share in the work of helping and
healing. I was received with expressions of
pleasure, and one said to me : "We are just in
need of help from one in your state of advance-
ment. There is a home near here where the
life lived seems a beautiful one to some of
us, and repulsive to others. *You* know what

true beauty is; tell us if the repulsiveness is in the home we speak of, or in ourselves."

Then they made me see, as in a vision, this home; I followed in spirit the lives of its inhabitants, and I saw that the ugliness was caused by want of true insight in the observer. Yes; we dare not here endeavour to help another until we are sure that he needs that help; often we find that there is a beam in our own eye, rather than a mote in his. I now began to see more clearly that knowledge was not a thing of the intellect at all, and I returned home humbler and wiser. There is no need to go here and there to seek for work, it lies at one's right hand, ready whenever there is sufficient daylight in our spirit to enable us to work aright. Truly it is often night with us when no man can work.

You will see by what I have said about "Schools" that, though they resemble in a few points your universities, art schools, and unions

of men for kindred purposes, yet we learn and
work in other ways from yours ; ways that may
seem less direct, but are really the truest. We
do not separate art from life, beauty from the
soul, nor do we separate work from beauty or life
from art. The outer and inner correspond, and
we only know any art really when we have
translated it into action.

There are also many communities for other
purposes ; for cultivating the earth : for though
always beautiful, because unstained, yet it is
barren in some directions, and needs culture that
it may yield delight to the psychic senses. We
are not obliged to go to all such centres, for
if need be, we can be taught much by others who
cause true pictures to arise before our vision, so
that we can see all the processes, and then put
them into action. Nor are we confined to those
with whom we live for fellowship and intercourse.
It is true we have both more fully with them ;
but if need arises I can be made to hear and see

what goes on in any sphere, and can communicate and be communicated with. Then again, we listen with delight to the talks and ripe experience of some whose nature it is to give out to his fellows ; some one who on earth, probably, was a poet or a preacher. He, in speaking to us can see exactly the effect produced upon us by his words, and he directs and modifies his speech accordingly : we answer him, as it were, without interrupting him, and he need therefore never be out of harmony with his audience.

RELATIONSHIP OF ONE COMMUNITY TO ANOTHER : GOVERNMENT, ETC.

We are not isolated units here, with merely individualistic needs and desires : rather do we live under different governments, answering somewhat to your different nations. Two characteristics of earthly governments are, however, eliminated : *e.g.*, all interference on the part of any, and all wilful misconduct. Our methods resemble

F

an ideal patriarchal government. The father in
experience and wisdom advises, protects, and
instructs those who are related to him in pyschic
bonds ; that is in character and bent of the soul,
but who are yet young and tender in the new
life. All force, all necessity, all tyranny are
absent, and one is guided or controlled most
willingly or not at all. There is no possible
place for punishment of any kind ; to such as
may in any way transgress the divine law there
comes a sense of separation, which lasts until the
faculties of the soul are readjusted. The old
myth of the Tower of Babel is re-enacted ; for
where there is not harmony of purpose, there
confusion of language comes, and we do not
understand each other's speech ; while, on the
contrary, when all goes well, all will hear in their
own language, whoever the speaker may be.

Just as the eye, the ear, and the palate choose
and prefer some things to others, so the soul
senses draw us to such things and people as can

give us pure joy, or cause us to grow in the most healthy way possible.

When the Master was living his earthly life, your world, ours, and the next, all lay open to him much more fully than to most. There was so much in his nature that responded to heavenly influences, and so little to obstruct, that he may be said to have lived in all three at different periods of the same life. This "openness" of his is clearly shown in the story of his life, for the power was so abundant that even those around could not help sharing: they heard voices, they saw the heavenly messengers like birds descending: they saw the psychic body shine through the physical. The Master, then, knew enough of our life to promise to his disciples that if they fulfilled certain conditions they should attain certain planes of being. If they followed and obeyed—not a person, but those inner principles which belong to humanity —then they would be fit to lead others. So

those who govern here are not the great ones
of the earth, nor yet those who have been dis-
tinguished for great intellectual gifts : they are
those men or women who, whatever position
they may have filled, have been truest to their own
nature, obeying the law within, without that
parleying with the inner voice which leads to
self-deception and crooked ways. Such govern
and are as fathers to those who need help ; while
to others who need it not, there is as much freedom as if they existed alone in the universe.

We begin, then, generally as children, and
gradually grow up to independent maturity ; we
become as fathers ; we pass on to other worlds,
while others take our vacant places.

Thus the law of change is still universal : the
flowers change from one beauty to another, or
disappear from our view to reappear in other
forms : the earth changes and beautifies under
our faithful labour ; our friends grow in spirit and
sometimes they too pass away ; our work, our

thought,change and pass from one order to another.
A simple, natural life is ours with the sanctified
will as the motive power ; no machinery, no
tools, no storehouse or barns; we are clothed upon
as the lilies are ; we gather the fruit for our healing straight from the tree of life. To those who
are out of harmony with this divine order this
earth may often seem a wilderness, and the pools
of living water like dreary wastes of sand : but
this is only while their hour of tribulation lasts ;
only until they yield themselves to the law of
their being, and become united, one, a whole
creation. Our joys and sorrows, our trials and
triumphs, lie closely together, as they do in your
world ; but the joys are greater, and the triumphs
more just and unsullied. We put our lower
nature in its proper place of subjection under our
feet, and thus ruling it we rise to perfect manhood, and share the throne of all perfect
humanity ; and then we rise by-and-by to greater
heights and share the throne of the Divine.

RELIGION.

" I believe in one God."
" I am the Son of God."
' I know that my Redeemer liveth."

In speaking of this subject I use the word
" religion " in its widest sense, and include in it
not only the true and inner religion of the heart,
but also the outward forms and creeds.

When men have passed the " article of death,"
and have gone through the first stages of this
life and emerged from the mental confusion
consequent on their change of environment, then
naturally to most must come a readjustment of
their religious faith. To nearly all the surroundings in which they find themselves are immensely
different from what they had expected ; conse-
quently there is a great change in their mental
attitude.

This will be specially the case with two
orders of minds : the atheistical and the orthodox.
By the orthodox I mean those of any creed or

nation whose religion is a matter of creed, of doctrine : those to whom the letter of the law is more important than the spirit.   To the atheist,— finding that his individuality has survived and passed beyond the physical plane,—there comes naturally the thought, that perhaps. immortality may not be the idle dream he once believed it to be.   The orthodox, finding himself neither in the heaven he expected to go to (whether that heaven was a spiritual or a sensual one), nor in the hell he thought his enemies would enter, naturally drops much of his old wordy, musty creed, and begins to lay hold on more spiritual principles.

Of course, we who were brought up in the Christian religion expected to see God on a white throne with the Saviour seated beside him.   But you know that this was a mistake.   We have no means of proving the existence of God other than you have : we'neither see nor handle the Invisible; there is no possibility of outward proof that God is ! Our faith rests on the intuitions of our deepest spirit, on the needs of our being, and on our reason ; but of any tangible proof we have none.

How is it then, you will ask, with regard to the one we call Master ; have not our friends told us that they have seen Him and have had their spirits go out to him in adoration ? Yes, that is true, but I cannot prove to you that the One who produced that effect on me is more than myself. There are many here who deny that He is any more than a spirit manifesting in soul-form like their own. They say that all who are here have passed over from the earth within the last hundred years. "Thou art not yet fifty years old, and how makest thou thyself then older than our fathers ! "

So you must understand that everything here that is not purely psychic (answering to your physical) is a matter of belief, and not of actual proof.

Thus you will see that religious belief here

springs from much the same sources that it does with you, except that with us it does not depend on what we have been taught or have heard from others ; religion is for each, whatever form it may take, the real and sincere outcome of the inner state. For myself and those most closely related to our sphere, I have already told you what we hold to be the truth with regard to God and Man, and we also believe that this becomes the faith of most, if not all, sooner or later. But at first there is great variety of creed. Some believe that this state,—which we speak of as a passing and intermediate one,—is final. They say : " We always knew that man had a double nature ; that the physical was not all ; our mistake was in thinking that his higher nature was fully developed on earth. We see that here those higher powers have full play, therefore we are now complete, and this state is the final one. Let us, then, devote these powers to humanity, and do all we can to help our brethren to make the best of this new and brighter world."

Such people often lead beautiful, self-sacrificing lives here, for they work with the energy of those who believe that the day is short and the night is at hand.

Others, again, whose natures lie somewhat open on the spiritual side, but who are still bound in the old grave-clothes of injustice and selfishness believe, that to those only who have faith, an entrance into the heavenly spheres will be granted.

Some, looking backwards rather than forwards in their views of life and growth, believe that they will be re-incarnated on the earth from whence they came; such seek rather for their own perfection than for their union with the great stream of life, with each other and with the highest.

To some the worship of nature is sufficient, others seem to find all they need in the concentration of their faculties on their life and work; while others again who come over with their hearts full of faith in a personal God—a special Saviour for a favoured few—often endure great anguish of spirit, and cry: "They have taken away my Lord, and I know not where they have laid him!" But this anguish is the furnace in which all selfish egotism is burned away; and so by various paths we are led to true unity of thought, of life, and of essential being.

It is of course but a matter of small importance what form a man's religious views may take, or whether he has any at all; especially as we believe that in due time all will know the joy that now only some possess. James was quite right when he defined religion as personal holiness and self-sacrificing love. In this life the law of our being is, first, that we should sorrow for failure in past or present; failure to reach our highest ideal whatever that ideal may be; and then next that we should seek to live not unto ourselves, but for our brethren.

MARRIAGE.

We have said that some here do not care for
the counterpart of your home life. That may be
because the habits of mind and the character
with which they come over are opposed to it ;
but still with all there must be some choice of
companionship, some affinity with one more than
another, and to most the special companionship
of one is almost a necessity for the happy development of their being. This is specially a
characteristic of modern and western nations.
Such companionship is a blessed thing, and is
the true marriage of which the earthly is only a
broken shadow. But there is one great point
of difference. This marriage is not necessarily
between those who, on earth, were of an opposite
sex ; the body is cast off, and the psyche knows
nothing of male or female. All are one in their
great Head, the Head of the whole human family,
the most perfect Man. It is the two types of ,
character which on earth are generally masculine

and feminine that are best suited to become one in spirit; therefore, it is not strange that real union on earth should often be continued here, though it is not necessarily nor always so. Here the great power of insight that we have into each other's true being prevents mistakes; and the affections and the reason being united, all discord and disappointment are prevented. Yet occasionally we see some grow in such different ways that they fall apart, but without any bitterness. These unions are unions of perfect responsiveness and sympathy: each can speak more fully to the other, and cause to be heard or seen by them all the beautiful visions that they have. A greater power both of giving and receiving constitutes the bond.

"I Saw the Holy City, New Jerusalem."

You may by this time have gained the impression that we have described our life as a strange mixture of natural and spiritual; we have spoken of houses, lands, clothes, food, books; and on the other hand have spoken of the will power as the great creative agency, of soul-impressions rather than bodily senses.

That impression would be in the main a correct one ; for our life here is a mingling of the old and the new ; the past and the present ; not yet wholly spirit, nor wholly of earth, we partake of both natures. Like a girl who is just between childhood and womanhood may be a child one day and a woman the next ; or like a dragon-fly just emerging from its case comes out with wings, it is true, but they are folded ones, and for a time that bears some proportion to his short life he seems rather to crawl on these folded wings, as if he were a grub, than to open them and fly away.

Our pleasures and our duties are never separated here as they sometimes are with you. There is no such thing as a pleasure disconnected from work, or growth, or duty ; neither is there any beauty disconnected from true life, nor any idle sorrow or grief that is not distinctly healing in its effect, cleansing or raising the soul. There is no weariness, such as comes from mere ennui, or from a vacant mind : real honest fatigue of the body comes only from the imperfection of the growing soul, not yet strong enough to bear all the strain put on it by its spirit lord.

In your world you have the visible, physical life in all stages of development, and in all forms ; the rock, the flower, the animal, and the man. You have also mental life in all stages, from the simplest animal instinct, to the most complex brain of man. So in our world we have the psychic life in all stages : that life which may be said to be outward and visible to our psychic senses. We have also the spirit life ; unseen except in its outcome, as it manifests itself through the psychic.

Thus we have trees and stones, animals and man ; all with the same kind of life running through them, but not to the same degree. How would this world appear to you, if you could enter it in your present body? The old simile of the fish and the bird would be true. The fish that sees, breathes, and flies through the water could not change with the bird; the air would be too strong for him; and his powers, so perfect in themselves, could not adjust themselves to their new surroundings. You are the fish, and we are the bird. You would find our air too strong for you, and we should find yours too heavy for us. We enter into your world only through its reflected, but true soul-form; we see the pictures of earthly things reflected in you, as you see things reflected by and on the eye.

Imagine yourself, however, over here, and with the help of what we have told you try to "see" the new world. I think the first sensation would be of surprise that it is so much like your own: what would first strike you would be the resemblance : town and country, sea and grass ; flowers and fruit ; men and women and children ; life and motion. But the differences would soon begin to press upon your notice. The absence of all dirt, sordid misery, haggard and over-burdened faces, and savage and sin-sodden countenances. Sorrowful ones you might see ; grave faces as well as bright, shining, outgoing looks ; you would see people at work of various kinds, but anything resembling the whip of the taskmaster would be absent. Weariness might occasionally be noticed, but not impatience or despair.

Perhaps the next thing you would notice would be the close fellowship you would have with all forms of nature around you, and your power over what we call the lower : power for your good, but not for the injury of anything. The air you breathe out, for instance, is no longer poisoned for your brother's use ; the grass you walk on is not trodden down and spoiled for

G

other feet ; the flowers you gather do not leave
bleeding stalks behind them to wither and become
unpleasing to the eye.

The sea will no longer divide, or be an instrument of death, but rather a friend if only you
trust yourself to it. The mountain will no longer
be a barrier for toilsome and dangerous climbing,
but a friend from whose surface you may see a
wider stretch of the new country. All things
will be "very good" to you if you let your nature
have full play, and live according to its simple
laws.

Should you hear music, you would find an
answering strain rise up within your being. You
might look in vain for any instrument from which
the strains could have proceeded, but instead of
an organ, the player would play upon the strings
of your inner being, and they would respond
fully and perfectly to his touch.

Then again there is a great difference in the
way you converse with those you meet. At first

you would naturally use your own language or seem to do so as in a dream (let us say). As you were understood and answered, it would seem as if they also spoke the same language, but in a little while you would see that it was not the outward language which they comprehended and replied to, but that you made them feel your meaning, and they, in return, impressed their thoughts upon you.

Thus you would find in a hundred ways that the old was passing away, and that all things were becoming new.

And so the soul—
When it is freed at last from earthly bonds,
Flies from its prison house to its true home.
On earth it was encumbered, incomplete,
Dumb and half blind, struggling with earth and sin ;
Striving and groping on its darkened way ;
With the eternal question on its lips
Eternally unanswered—" Why ?'
Until the angel comes with outstretched wings,
 Dark underneath to him but light above ;)
That angel which like two-faced Janus stands,

One face for ever turned towards the past,
The other forward to the life to come;
That dreaded messenger from the Unseen
Who is called Death by you, but Life by us.

When we speak of growth, of childhood and manhood, of course we do not mean a growth in days or in years. The psyche grows only in soul-ways; waxing strong in spirit; that is, there comes to the soul increased power of manifesting itself, a more varied and a fuller life. This growth is not always at the same rate; sometimes, indeed, the soul seems to remain stationary, or even to decline for a while: but speaking generally, progress is the law of the new nature as of the old. But there is not that failure of the powers that there is with you in old age. The soul, when it reaches the highest point of perfection, when it is truly matured, is prepared for another form of life, and departs to higher regions.

The time of our departure is not in any way fixed by our own will or sense of fitness.

Generally we become aware when our hour is at hand ; a higher power than our own, above us, yet in us, sweetly constrains us to depart. The body which we have then dissolves, disappears, is restored to the sphere from which it was taken, as your bodies (though much less quickly) return to the earth from which they were derived. Painlessly and naturally the tent is taken down ; the old earth and the old heaven vanish away, and the new heavens appear to us in all their spiritual beauty.

Thus we leave behind us no corrupting body to hurt or annoy, but fade away from the vision like a cloud. All that was psychic remains in the psychic sphere, and our spirits enter into the third state which has been called final, simply because we know nothing of what lies beyond it.

HARMONY OF NATURE.

The teaching you have already received on the harmony of nature may find a place here.

The word "nature" is used in the sense of outward, physical life.

To be at one with nature is, for nature to be able to impart to you all that it possesses that you need, and for you, in return, to be able to give it that care, attention, and cultivation which it needs to receive from your higher form of manifested life.

Between you and the food which nature supplies, the relationship is not yet sufficiently close for you to plant and have the certainty of reaping. No, there are all kinds of adverse influences which may come in to prevent you from reaping the perfect harvest. Again, there is a certain amount of discord between you and nature in many directions. You cannot, you dare not trust yourself absolutely to the water, lest you drown; the air is unable to support you when you seek to soar; the lightning, which should only strengthen the electrical forces of the body, may suddenly drive the life-principle out of it.

You fear the heights and the depths; the awful spaces in the firmament; and against the long courses of eternity you feel but as the insect of a day. But when the redemption of the body of manifested life is complete, then between you and nature will there be only the need to ask that you may receive; to seek and find; to knock and have it opened.

As far as this nature in its broadest sense can reach, all shall be yours, while on your side there will be the perfect knowledge and power so to deal with its forces, that you will give it the equivalent for that which it lends to you.

There is, more or less, the same discord in your own nature. Each part of that nature should only require what the other can give, and it should be given fully and freely. Each part should be perfectly controlled and balanced by the other. The flesh must not war against the spirit, but must freely give it what it needs: namely, the power of outward manifestation; and the spirit must not war against the flesh, but give to it all purifying and ennobling breath to fuse it into something divine.   All the latent powers of the whole man, even those wordless aspirations of the spirit, shall find immediate and full expression by and by ; and without fear and without failure all shall be one, and then truly shall God be all in all.

PART II.—THE PNEUMA.

INTRODUCTORY.

"And I was caught up into the third heaven, and heard things *impossible* to utter."

IT is with some amount of uncertainty, dear friends, that we start upon the second part of our communications. For if we have had difficulty in finding words that should convey to you tolerably true pictures of our life here, we shall have still more difficulty when we have ourselves to be taught by those with whom we also have no common language. How far we shall be successful will be seen later on.

There is much symmetry in the way in which our Bible begins and closes ; and if I speak of this book it is not only because it is so well-known to us both, but because of all religious books (many of which are as truly inspired as ours), the Bible is best suited to our order of mind.

The Bible begins with the history of physical man, while as yet his higher nature (eternal in its true essence) lay dormant and unmanifested within him. It is here we see those powers which man shares with the animal at their highest : courage, patience, and a certain fierce battling for himself and his family ; while the longer years he lived were partly owing to the physical being supreme. Here, too, we see the rise of the intellectual powers (as distinct from the moral), in the works and inventions of that old race.

In the last book we have the true history of the psyche. Put from you the idea that John's revelation is one of mere future events ; a prophesy in the sense of foretelling things to come. It is rather the inner history of the human ego in his second and third states ; that is as soul and spirit in the sense in which we have so often used those words.

It is a wonderful picture of life ; of yours and mine, and of that of all either in one state or another. It begins after the introductory part of the messages to the churches, and to understand it you must have two leading ideas in your mind, which if once clear to you will make the whole book, we believe, intelligible to you and also introduce better the spirit life we are about to describe.

The two threads are these: you have here the *perfect* man, and you have the *imperfect*, and the history of these two runs side by side. The perfect man is represented in many ways and under many titles, all of which titles have their deep meaning, and show different sides of a perfect character. Although all these are supposed to refer to the Christ whom John knew—and indeed are true of him—yet they must not be limited in that way, for they refer to the type ; to that perfect being which was from eternity and shall be to eternity, and who is therefore well spoken of as the First and the Last. We, indeed, are as yet only a little way on that road which leads to perfect manifestation, but we came from the Complete One, and we shall return to Him : if He has all wisdom—the seven spirits of God—it is only as head of the race ; such wisdom is the birthright of all, and shall be theirs when the set time is at hand.

We have, then, in this book the human soul in all stages of development compared and contrasted with one who has gone through such discipline and has come forth—perfect Man and perfect Son of God.

The soul begins his conscious history, generally, in this way : If he believes in God it is as a being of infinite power, who lives apart from his creation—on a throne—and whose attributes are represented by thunder and lightning, while all nature bows down before him in passive awe. This is the time when courage, power, and all physical qualities are his ideal.

And, behold, a throne was set in Heaven, and one sat on the throne. And out of the throne proceeded lightnings and thunderings and voices. And four-and-twenty elders, and four living creatures were round about the throne, and they rest not day nor night, saying, Holy, holy, holy, Lord God Almighty, which was, and is, and is to come. Thou art worthy, O Lord, to receive glory and honour and power : for thou hast created all things, and for thy pleasure they are and were created.—Rev. iv., 2-11.

The next stage in his life may be this : He begins to feel pressing on him the awful mysteries of his being ; life is a closed book to him, the eternal " Why " begins to rise within him, and at the same time he feels himself unable and unworthy to open the book.

Then he is happy if he learns to believe that there is one who has both the power and the will to reveal these mysteries to him. One, not a being apart from himself, but who is only a little further on in the way of experience: one, who is both the Lion and the Lamb ; who unites all the strength of the divine with the beauty of self sacrifice.

And I saw a book sealed with seven seals. And no man in heaven, nor in earth, neither under the earth was able to open the book, neither to look thereon. I beheld, and, lo, in the midst of the throne, stood a Lamb as it had been slain. And he came and took the book out of the right hand of him that sat upon the throne.— Chap. v., 1-7.

This true, perfect man breaks the first seal, and the soul becomes conscious of new powers. Strong in faith, in the greatness of humanity, he goes forth conquering, and to conquer.

When the Lamb opened one of the seals, I saw, and behold a white horse ; and he that sat on him had a bow and a crown, and he went forth conquering and to conquer.—Chap. v., 1-2.

Another seal is broken: his experience widens; but this time it is not the triumphant march of the conquerer, but the cry of defeat; while he learns through loss and through conflict, through the wounds of sin and the loss of self-esteem how to conquer in a truer way.

When he had opened the second seal there went out another horse that was red: power was given to him that sat thereon to take peace from the earth.—Rev. vi., 3 and 4.

A third seal is broken: he learns that there is no distinction between the earthly and the heavenly: the corn and the wine are as sacred as the angel's words or the sound of the heavenly trumpets: he learns something of the unity of life.

When he had opened the third seal, I beheld a black horse; and he that sat on him had a pair of balances in his hand. And I heard a voice say, A measure of wheat for a penny, and three measures of barley for a penny ; and see thou hurt not the oil and the wine.—Chap. vi., 5 and 6.

The fourth seal shows us how, through the loss of whatever may have been as dear to him as life itself, he is led on to a higher plane, the plane of self sacrifice.

When he had opened the fourth seal, I looked, and behold a pale horse ; and his name that sat on him was Death, and Hell followed with him. And power was given them over the fourth part of the earth, to kill with sword, and with hunger, and with death, and with the beasts of the earth.— Chap. vi., 7 and 8.

The fifth seal shows him in that phase of experience when there presses on him a sense of injustice, because the righteous seem to suffer and the wicked to prosper. "How long, O Lord, before thou wilt avenge thy saints?"

When he had opened the fifth seal, I saw under the altar the souls of them that were slain for the

word of God: and they cried with a loud voice,
saying, How long, O Lord, dost thou not judge
and avenge our blood? And it was said unto
them that they should rest for a little season.—
Chap. vi., 9-11.

The sixth seal shows the soul's dread of death
and of what lies beyond it.

When he had opened the sixth seal there was a
great earthquake ; the sun became black, and the
moon became as blood; the stars of heaven fell
and the heaven departed, and every mountain and
island were moved out of their places. And all
men hid themselves in the dens and the rocks of
the mountains ; and said, Fall on us, and hide us
from the face of him that sitteth on the throne, and
from the wrath of the Lamb : for the great day
of his wrath is come ; and who shall be able to
stand ?—Chap. vi., 12-17.

And so he is led on until—at the seventh seal,
there is silence in heaven: that is, his mind is

H

calmly poised on the great foundation truths, and
he can wait for joy or sorrow, conflict or peace,
with sure and steadfast faith that all is well, and
well for ever and for all.

*And when he had opened the seventh seal, there
was silence in heaven about the space of half an
hour.*—Chap. viii., 1.

The seven trumpets carry on this history of
the man on a more spiritual plane ; like an artist
who becomes a sculptor, he has learnt much that
will help him, but he must apply it in different
ways, for soul-battles are not fought once and for
all, but have to be re-fought on a different battle-
ground and with new weapons. For is it not
true in our life that the old doubts and difficulties
which we thought dead rise again in greater
strength, and must be met and conquered in the
new spirit that has been born within us.

The seven vials show the history of those who
have more struggle, more apparent discord to

overcome ; such as are led through fire, rather than through green valleys. Yet all will finally sing the same triumphant song of victory over what has been out of harmony with their divine nature : the victory of life over death, of holiness over sin, the dissolving of all that is not truly spiritual, and the manifestation of the new man with the new name.

The vision of the throne is now of the throne of God and the Lamb ; that is God and Man made one for ever.

Such, dear friends, is your history and ours : it may be lived out on your plane, or on ours ; but somewhat after this is the experience of the soul before it enters the third life, of which we will now try to speak.

THE TRANSITION.

We have spoken several times about our communications with the life beyond ours, and of our visits to that better country. Such visits are but visionary, and the communications difficult. We do not really enter the next state until we leave this psychic world behind us for ever. Our psychic bodies are no more suited to live there than your bodies are for this world. When we have "gone" (as we say), it has been that our spirits might be strengthened or enlightened in ways that were not possible here, or that we might get insight into some duty not intelligible otherwise. We see "in a glass darkly," and not "face to face."

Now, what happens when our time comes to depart? It is this: our psychic form dissolves, fades away, is folded up, is dissipated into the sphere from which it was taken, leaving our spirit free to pass beyond into purer and rarer air more fitted for it. There is no pain or struggle in such a dissolution, nor any break in consciousness. Our friends bid us farewell for a time, but we need not say farewell to them, for we shall see and know them more intimately even than before.

Their eyes may not perceive us, but our clearer vision will embrace the past as well as the present, the old as well as the new.

(All that we have now to tell you has been given us by our spirit friends).

Man is now pneuma or spirit; not that pure, invisible, immortal essence of which we have spoken, but approaching more closely to it. The true, the real man yet remains hidden from comprehension; the final, the deepest mystery of all.

It is not simply that he has taken off two coverings, the physical and the psychical, and is now himself, unclothed upon. Rather he manifests himself in three ways at different times and in different degrees: in body, in soul, and in spirit. The physical and the psychical bodies have been cast off and left in the spheres to which they belonged; he has now a spiritual body, while yet the true man has been complete through all. The body of the body, the body of the soul, are gone for ever, and he is now clothed upon with the body of the spirit.

THE HIGHER LIFE.

" On the earth the broken arcs,
In the heaven a perfect round."

Before we try to describe the spirit body and its functions, it will be well to speak of the new sphere in which the Man is now manifesting. This sphere is not one and single as the intermediate is, but is seven spheres closely connected together.

Perhaps a diagram will make this clearer.

The three central are the Unity Spheres; the side ones are the Duality Spheres.*

---

* The connecting lines should be red to indicate the stream of life. The Unity Spheres blue, for purity and perfection. The Duality black, for conflict, etc.

THE DIAGRAM.

I. The first Unity Sphere. Introductory, for strengthening and improving the character and . the new powers.

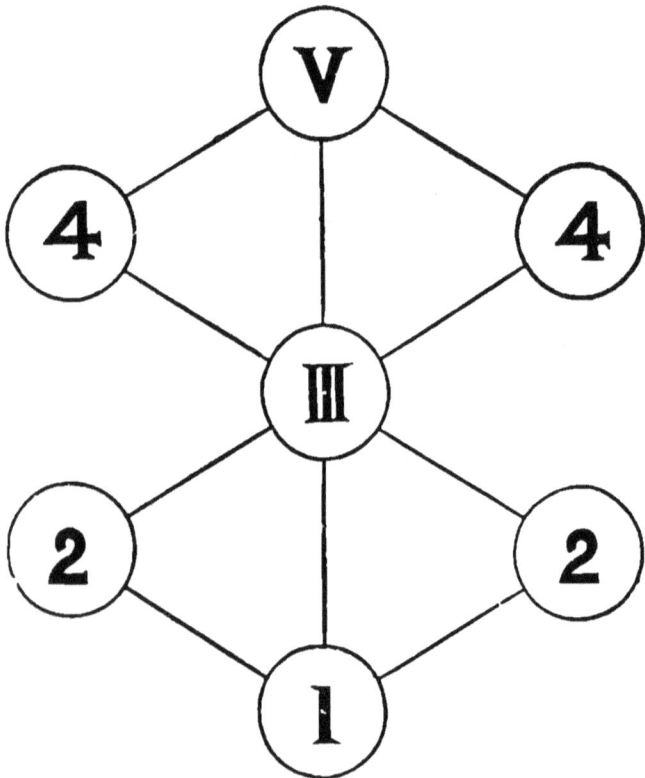

III. The second Unity Sphere. For action and exercise of powers.

V. Third Unity Sphere. Peace ; rest ; the equipoise of the perfectly manifested being.

2. The first Duality Spheres. Discipline : the growth, guidance and strengthening of such parts of the being as were still weak and imperfect.

4. Second Duality Spheres. Discipline on a higher plane : the completion of the work. The man now passes into the last Unity Sphere, the sphere of perfection, and beyond that who shall say! Certainly we know nothing.

The Duality Spheres are so called, chiefly because the old double consciousness (which is almost dormant in the Unity Spheres) is again in force. In force, that is, in the sense of conflict of one part of our nature with another ; not merely in the ability to think of ourselves as if we were two beings. This double consciousness is revived in the dual spheres because it is then easier for the ego to see its own weaknesses ; to condemn and struggle against them.

Thus these spheres are dual as being in pairs; dual in the divided experience, and above all dual as to the double consciousness.

The unity are so called, not only or chiefly because they are the one sphere for all, but because there this unity of consciousness is existent.

The unity of the whole seven in one is shown in the oneness of the man's manifestation; through all he dwells in his spirit-body; through all he is a man of seven dimensions until he comes to the perfection of his being, as far as we can judge of perfection.

No spirit, we believe, ever passes through more than one of each of the two spheres marked 2 and 4: that is he goes to the right or to the left, but not to both. (The words rights and left, of course, are used only in reference to the diagram.)

What, then, causes him to enter one of these spheres rather than the other? It is the bent of

his deep soul-character.   There is no uniformity
in mankind, rather there is infinite diversity.   Yet
it divides, broadly speaking, into two classes, call
them by what name you please, say :

    The religious and the scientific :

    The imaginative and the practical :

    The introspective and the outlooking.

Now, the soul that has the one bent passes into
the opposite sphere, that his nature may be so
cultivated and disciplined that he shall be a
perfect and not a one-sided being.

When we speak of perfect and imperfect I
think you understand our meaning.   Sin—as you
know it—that is a wilful failure to do the thing
that is known to be right, or the equally wilful
doing of the wrong, sin, I say, is left behind
finally in the psychic.   By perfect I mean the
essential being fully manifested, and by imperfect
we mean not fully manifested.   Man, then, is not
perfect until he reaches the 7th sphere; the
Unity in Peace.

Man thus passes through only five of the
seven spheres, but the seven are so closely connected by a constant stream of life circling
through all, that he may be said to inhabit
them all.

Finally the three unity spheres are specialised
thus :

I.—Is that state where all the qualities
developed in the physical life reach their highest
stage.

III.—The same, only psychical.

V.—The perfection of the pneumatic.

And now with what words can we describe
the spirit-body? It is not like unto the physical
or the psychical. It is not an etherealized earthly
body, yet it resembles it in one point, it manifests
the real man in various ways. You manifest
yourself by speech and look, and perceive others
by the touch and the ear. So the spirit has its
spirit-vision, hearing, speech, etc.

VISION.

This is that true, deep, spirit intuition into the realities of things of which you, no doubt, have had glimpses in your earthly life. That piercing eye of the soul which lays bare the roots, the deep foundations of things.

Peter had this for a moment when he "saw" Christ and exclaimed "Thou art the Son of God;" saw that is not the outward Jesus of Nazareth, nor the outwardly manifested character of a leader of men, but the real, true, perfect, human soul. He lost this power shortly afterwards, and so misunderstood his master, that the latter, thrown back upon himself after being for a moment truly "seen"—lost his own spirit equipoise, his true vision, and misinterpreted Peter seeing him as an adversary, when he was truly a friend, though a mistaken one.

Spirit vision always looks to the roots of things; below the righteous action it looks for truth; below the generous, for justice : and below

all for love, which is life in its highest manifestation.

The physical sees the sun and stars, and perceives that the sun gives heat and life, day and
night, etc.

The psychic sees the laws which govern these
suns, and knows that they are good.

The spirit vision sees the life which produces
the laws and causes them all to be, and to be
perfect.

Again: the physical sees the rich man pulling
down his barns and building larger ones, and
perceives that it is that he may have room where
to bestow his goods.

The psychic sees why he does this; that he
may say to his soul: Eat, drink and be satisfied.

The pneuma perceives that the spring of these
actions is injustice: the man not being perfectly
just (or rather justice not being perfectly manifested in him), fears to trust himself to nature:
fears that he will suffer real loss in the stress of

life or in the pangs of death, and hopes that he may by his own lower powers get to himself more than others, a shelter from the forces he fears instead of trusts. He knows not that he is endowed with a birthright, as son of God, of which nothing can possibly deprive him.

When we were speaking of the psychic vision we said that it was strictly limited to such " objects," to such perceptions as would be helpful to the man, or present to him some quality of the soul with which he was in harmony and which he could, therefore, see. Also we said that (the limitations of time and space still fettering him to some extent) he could only see things apart from his surroundings by having them impressed on him by a power outside himself. With the spirit vision these limitations do not exist, or not to the same degree. The vision, like a circle, holds all things within itself, and its gaze pierces equally to the distant or the near, to the past or the present. You remember the past, and memory and imagination can reproduce it in a more or less broken manner, but the spirit sees the past as you do the present, as really and as truly. When we say all things are within its range, we must remind you that we use the word "all" in a limited way. By "all" we mean the whole of the psychic life of the ego. The future is still a sealed book, though greater powers of intuition enable it to read even that more clearly than before. Still, in the sense of knowing future events as we know the past, we use the word "sealed."

Elisha must have had the psychic vision when he saw Gehazi on his deceitful errand; but Christ had the spirit vision when from his intimate knowledge of the character of Judas he said: "This is he who shall betray me."

The physical sees the besieged city with the prophet within its walls; the psychic sees the chariots and horses of the Lord encircling it in the hour of danger, to leave it when that special need is past: the spirit sees the love and pity, the just and abiding care that is for ever around —not only that city, but the army of the besiegers and the whole world.

The spirit-eyes, then, see the spirit-forms and the world in which they dwell, but it sees far more than this : it sees Reality under Appearance, and Truth beneath any veil.

Nor is there any confusion arising from this vast field of vision, for the harmony of the spheres is so great that the eye takes in all, or a part, as easily as your eye takes in an extended landscape or a minute object.

HEARING.

Hearing is vision looked at from a slightly different point of view. When any faculty is in motion, is being exercised, the spirit hears it, and it is to him the highest and truest form of music; when the faculty is at rest, then the eye sees it, and it is to him the highest form of Art ; true painting and true sculpture.

Hearing is also not confined to the present : the past, back to the soul's first dwelling in flesh is 'audible' to the spirit-ear. Further back than that in the soul's history remains to be unfolded in the higher spheres : the seventh chiefly.

SPEECH.

Speech is constant, or at least tends towards continuity. It is the outward expression of the spirit, therefore it is constant like the expression on a man's face, which is the outcome of his constant character. When a spirit is purified and becomes "holy," that is one, united in himself— he ceases not to cry day and night, "Holy, holy, holy." Not holy am I, but holy art thou, O Lord, towards whom my being ever tends.

TIME AND SPACE.

"And Time shall be no more."

"And when they say Lo, here ! or lo, there ! go not forth : for the Divine Logos is nigh thee, even in thine heart."

What has already been said about vision will

I

prepare us to understand the conditions of time and space. The man is now becoming a seven-dimensional being, and the old fetters of time and space are falling from him rapidly. The psyche found no time long in the sense of weary-ing, nor short in the sense of incompetency to do his work : the pneuma is no longer conscious of time, he does not seem to be controlled by it in the least. The past and the present are merged in the eternal " Now," and the hither and thither are merged in the " Here am I," which is the spirit's constant response to the voice of his fore-runner and God. Yesterday and to-day are both alike to him, equally real, equally present. Through this he has power, as it were, to undo the wrongs of the past, so that more fully and truly than before, those things of which his true self might be eternally ashamed are rectified, and the stain washed away in the blood (which is the life) of his spirit.

So he sees and hears the complete sum of past

and present ; both are one and indivisible. He neither goes nor comes any more than love or pity goes or comes ; all of which he is cognizant is included within the circle of his being : it lies in his breast as the whole universe lies in the breast of the Highest.

UNITY.

" There is one God.
I and my Father are one."

Hail to thee, my brother !
   Friend of heart and soul :
Father, sister, mother,
   Part and yet the whole.
In the past I knew thee,
   When thou wast a flower
On my stem I bore thee,
   Blossom of an hour.
In the " Now " behold me
   Hidden in thy breast ;
In the life around thee,
   Both as host and guest.
I and thou transfigured,
   Thou and I become ;
Unity prefigured,
   For we two are one.

We have already explained why the unity spheres are so called. The unity consists in the reconcilement of man with himself, and in the first unfoldings of the true oneness of his nature.

Man in his earthly stage is often, if not always conscious of warring elements in himself, of opposing forces which are sometimes so evenly balanced that he cannot control one by the other, but is torn by the conflicting powers. Paul has stated this experience so fully and clearly that his words must always be the text-book on this subject. It is not the power of thinking of ourselves as of a separate entity that now passes away, but it is the discord that is merged in harmony, and the sense of impotency that vanishes, being replaced by the strength that comes from this true unity. The consciousness that we cannot do the good we wish, nor refrain from the weakness that we despise—this it is that saddens our earthly life, and makes us at times think we are only mortal and human, instead of

immortal and divine. All such discords pass
away in the unity spheres : the spirit was being
prepared for it in the Hades state, for there it
found the " will " could do much, now it can do
all things. " United to me ye can do all things,
severed from me ye can do nothing." Be at one
with true manhood and all things are possible,
but severed from the true and living vine ye can
do nothing.

It is true that the man, though at peace with
himself, is not yet perfect : there are still many
traits to be developed, and perchance some evil
yet to be burned away : how, then, can there be
this concord ; has light any agreement with
darkness ? We believe it is this way :—The
imperfect and undeveloped parts of his being
are in abeyance, and remain so for awhile until
he passes into the next sphere ; while those
parts that are " ripe " are strengthened and
brought into play. So the words of John, or
rather of Jesus to John, may be understood.

"He that is holy, he that is righteous and he that is filthy, let him be so still." That is, if I am not yet thoroughly clean or true ; or again, if I am holy but not yet truly loving I do not become so here, in this sphere, but other qualities are being tested and strengthened, and the fire of deep experience will burn away the dross in good time. All that is evil is left without the gates of the city, and the man, perhaps bereft of his right hand or his right eye (for a time) enters into the city where nothing can defile, and where all tears are wiped away.

This is the time, or rather this is the point in the soul's history spoken of in John's revelation, when evil is bound for a thousand years, and when the redeemed part of the man enters the perfect state (typified by the 144,000 who wear white robes): while that part which is yet imperfect remains in abeyance, and is spoken of as cast into the fire, or left without the gates of the city. The perfection, you will understand, is partial, though complete as far as it goes. There comes a pause in the conflict with the evil and discordant elements, and in the calm and sunlight of this peace he grows and is strengthened rapidly.

We find it is easier to say what he is not, or what he does not than to describe him as he really is ; for your words are insufficient and sometimes misleading, and our knowledge is but scanty. But you will gather from what has been said, that he has not those alternations of power and weakness that you have and we have. We, for instance, see some things at some times, and may be said to be alternately seeing and blind : he sees all, and that continuously. He does not hear and not hear, but is clair-audient.

Though he is no longer out of harmony with his surroundings, we do not imply that there is no conflict or growth : his powers may be taxed to their utmost, but not beyond ; the strength is always sufficient to the day, and he grows as a

plant might, the surroundings of which were perfectly suited to its needs. All his powers are
living, in motion, not intermittently but constantly : this is a very high development of life.

" My Father worketh hitherto, and I work."
" And God rested the seventh day."

So much (or so little), dear friends, as to the
pneuma's new powers, or the new development
of the old. Next, what shall we say as to his
work, his occcupation ; what does the pneuma do
in his new life ? Broadly speaking, nothing.

In your life (especially in its lower developments) action, outward working is discordant,
often laborious, noisy, inefficient or rather impo-
tent. When action is united to the reason and
affections it becomes a higher and nobler thing,
but you know well that it is only the spirit put
into it that makes it anything but perfunctory and
transient. In the next state (in ours that is), the
will, the heart is supreme, and using at first out-

ward means it works on a higher plane and to nobler ends, until this new power, which we have called the will, gets more and more independent and needs no instrument, however nobly planned, through which to express its life and true self. In the "spheres" action as outward, or in the least degree differentiated from the being, has no place.

The spirit does not need to help his brother ; he *is* help. He does not love his neighbour, he *is* love. He does not show mercy ; he *is* mercy. No sun of benevolence shines in the city of his spirit ; he himself, the Lamb, the Man is the light thereof. No sea of cleansing pity breaks on the shore of his being, for he himself is pity. From his spirit's centre all rays go forth ; yet they are not cut off from him : the rays are himself and he is the rays. One does not say to his brother : I and thou ; for thou and I are one, and there is no difference.

Yet there is nothing vague, hazy, passionless

in this state; the man as he grows more and more into the God is not less alive, but more: the infinite contains in itself the finite, and the God has the man in his bosom.

This new being is well typified by the Seer who, when he wants to illustrate the vision speaks of the spirit as all eyes within and without, and when he speaks of motion and activity speaks of him as all wheels within wheels; that perfect circle of life whose centre is absolute rest.

Further, the pneuma does not make his environment, he and it are one. He does not make anything, he creates, and he is at once the creature and the creator. Again we must quote the pregnant words: " I and my Father are one."

THE TRUE MILLENIUM.

" And they shall reign with Him a thousand years."

It may perhaps seem illogical to speak of the length of time during which the spiritual man remains in the first unity sphere, for, as we have

said, the limitations of time are hardly felt by
him; but the period as it would seem to you, or
even to us, is about a thousand years. This is
the true millenium spoken of by John, when that
which is ready, ripe for transplanting into the new
world, goes there, and the yet undeveloped
remains dormant,—is bound in chains and cast
into the pit of oblivion. The seedlings of
character that are sufficiently grown are trans
planted into the new soil where they will grow
with increased vigour, and the backward and
weak ones are left for a while.

So the being at this stage may be likened to
an ellipse, rather than a circle; an oblate spheroid
like your earth, rather than a perfect sphere.

In the unity spheres the very atmosphere is
joy: sorrow is unknown: failure, doubt or disappointment: the life is like some mighty ocean
whose waters are ever drawn towards the fount
of life, and whose surface is untroubled by storms.
The evolution of such powers as are in motion

goes on in an ever forward, upward course; of such a state the saying is most true: " They shall hunger no more, neither thirst any more; neither shall the sun light upon them, nor any heat; for the Lamb which is in the midst of the throne shall lead them, and they shall reign for ever and ever."

(The " for ever " always refers to the particular state which is being spoken of, and is here that long period which we have supposed to be about a thousand years.)

A MESSAGE FROM THE FIRST UNITY SPHERE.

A mother to her daughter on earth.

Beloved.—I am going to try and let you see what my life is like here and now, that you may be able to hold communion with me, as I can with you, and may understand better what your destiny is. For time is short, and the longest life on earth or in Hades will seem but as a dream when you look back.

I am not merely your mother physically ; no,

there was entrusted to me, as to all mothers, though I was unconscious of it, a power, an influence, a stream of tendencies to hand on to you which should shape your whole being and your life. Had I been more faithful to the highest that I knew of, it would have been happier for me and easier for you. But it is not of that earthly life that I would speak now, nor must I dwell on my second life : it was quietly, tranquilly happy, but I did not develope through suffering and conflict some sides of my nature which are now feeble.

But to pass at once to my entrance here.

There came to me just before I left that former state a sudden call, a summons to gather all my powers and see in what I was deficient. It was a voice within me that seemed to say : "Art thou ready to depart?" I looked round and examined myself to see how it was with me. The calm peace that had filled my soul for so long was broken up, and I was troubled as I

looked in vain for many virtues which I thought
I had truly possessed for a long time.

No one accused me ; I was my own judge
and my own examiner.   I found that love was
too narrow, pity too self-centred, truth but partial.   Then the inner voice said, " Go forward ;
the weak shall be strengthened and the evil cut
away and cast into outer darkness ; go forward
into the light of a new day."

My soul then seemed to expand, to rise ;
or rather my spirit to break through my soul-
body like a conscious birth, and then instead
of light I found myself in utter darkness—
darkness such as I had never known before.
This darkness seemed to be empty (if I may so
express it), there was no sound, no thing, no
being.   I tried to speak but could not; to reach
out after something, no matter what ; all was
empty space.   But this was only for a moment.
I had been trying to hear and see with the old
psychic powers which I no longer possessed, and

my new born (not new created) spirit had not learned to use its new ones.

Then what a glorious change; light, life, music, beauty everywhere, a constant overflowing stream. I had been seeking outside what was within me; it was in my own breast that this new universe was lying, not away and apart from me.

You may think from what I say about looking within that we have no bodies here, but are pure spirit. That is not so; we have spirit bodies which are as much superior to our psychic bodies as they were to the physical. I cannot describe them to you at all clearly, but they are a real manifestation, a part of our being, and not mere clothing. We used to speak on earth of the three kingdoms of nature, and if you can, imagine our forms as embodying the strength and durability of the mineral, the beauty of the petals of a rose, and the conscious life of the animal, all combined. Or if you could unite the

lily and the rainbow with the soul looking forth
as from the eye of a man, you may get some
idea.

Then next I would say that our life is not a
mingling of joy and grief, of work and rest, as
the last was. I have known no sorrow, no
weariness, no inactivity of spirit since I have
been here, nor have I been conscious of any
such state of feeling in those around me.

When we were in the psychic world we were
conscious of being separated both from your
world and from this ; seeing only in vision or
broken fragments ; now the universe is always
open and undivided to us. We see all. (Not, of
course, material things.) By all I mean, that the
soul-life back to its manifestation in earthly
bodies and forward to the " now " in which we live
is open to us.

My children, for instance, are here with me
from their birth to the moment in which you
read this ; they are fully revealed and ever living

before me. Your past and your present are all
one, so that I know no difference between your
childhood and your youth, for the life is seen by
us as a perfect circle, and who shall say where it
begins or ends. The only difference is where the
pure gold of the circle is sometimes bright and
sometimes dull and tarnished with the clouds of
passing failure or sin.

. In the other life we first willed and then
acted ; we desired and then accomplished ; the
inner preceded the outer. Here there are not
two but one : we seem neither to think nor act,—
we are. I do not wish and then perform,—I am ;
there is no need to desire anything and then to
obtain it ; it is all within me and I have only to
breathe it out ; I have only just to *be* and all
things are included.

I know not if this will be at all clear to you,
or seem only words without meaning. Perhaps
if you will try to imagine me as more like in
nature what you believe God to be, then you will

K

get an impression which is as close to the reality as is possible.

I believe, beloved, that in this sphere no sadness, no unsatisfied desire is possible, but I also believe that there will come a time when we shall pass on, or when life will be different, and conflict may begin again in new forms.

One thing which I lacked when I passed over was love for others who were not near to me on earth. So I still am somewhat shut in with regard to many here, but I live in the life of my dear ones, making myself one with them, and seeking ever to draw their spirits towards the great fount of life, towards their Father and my Father.

We have but little sense of time here, nor do we realise the difference between far and near; there are no stops to our life in any way, but a great sense of infinite power, joy and blessedness which we are, rather than which we experience.

I have said that I had not the outgoing love to others not connected with my earthly life that I should have had. For this reason my union with those here is not complete, and they seem outside of myself, apart, rather than within. This restriction will last while I am in this sphere.

I would gladly tell you, if I could, how it is with my relationship with God and Christ. I know you have had some deep teaching from your friends as to the being of God ; but I must speak as my own experience has taught me. In the psychic world Christ was to me a teacher, a friend, a God, all united, and from Him my life and happiness seemed to spring. Here I see Him as still in the psychic world, with a body such as we all had there, and yet I am conscious that He is also here, and that from Him there goes out to me a constant stream of life, without which I feel I could not exist. I know that He is truly Man, only much further on in the great stream of existence than I ; but yet he is to me as I have said, all that I need to raise me from that lowness of nature which is death to the

K 2

highest life. It may be that God is to Christ what Christ is to me; I know not.

There is but little more that it would be possible for me to explain to you. We see all soul-forms, and that continuously: there is no darkness or emptiness.

We hear all soul-thoughts united in one grand harmony.

We know all soul-realities without forgetfulness and without mistake. Do not then imagine that I could ever be separated from you; your true being lies open before me, as mine will do to you when you have passed into this sphere.

Finally, beloved, remember that though your mother in some ways, I am your child, your sister in others: all relationships are included in one, so that you are mine and I am yours for ever.

I cannot sign this, for my new name is unspeakable.

CONCLUSION.

There is but little that we can tell you about the spheres beyond the first one. The names which we have given them will sufficiently indicate what they are.

After the rest and strengthening of the first unity sphere the man passes into one of the duality, and there conflict begins again on a higher plane. Those sides of his nature which have been dormant are now quickened into new life, and the spirit struggles to manifest himself more perfectly in all ways where he has been deficient. Then, greatly strengthened and enlarged, he passes into the Sphere of Action. We believe he then becomes the Creator rather than the creature ; more resembling the Lord God worshipped by the old Hebrews, but without the blemishes and limitations imputed by them to their ideal Creator.

The next conflict sphere is too remote to be clearly comprehended by us. Then comes, finally, the Unity in Peace, the highest which we can even faintly imagine. Here we must leave the spirit, for without some body, some manifested form he is to us, as to you, incomprehensible.

And now, dear friends, we must bring our little book to a conclusion. It has been to us throughout a source of true pleasure, and we believe that it will be to you, and to any who may read it both a guide and a friend. Once more we would say: Do not interpret us too literally; let the spirit of our words speak to your spirit. Also do not limit life by what we have told you, for there is much of which we have no knowledge, as well as much that we are not able to describe to you.

Our last words shall be :

Fear not.

Do not fear either Life or Death; for both are but the breath of the Divine.

Fear neither loss nor gain ; for the gain shall be for thy brother, and the loss shall only lighten thy burdens.

Fear not the mysteries of life ; for those mysteries are only the depths of thy own being, and the key to them all is Love.

Fear not the thorns upon thy pathway ; for they only protect the blossoms of thy heart.

Fear no anguish, no conflict ; for the cross is encircled with the crown of victory.

Fear nothing that unites thee to thy brethren; nothing that enables thee to understand and support thy weaker children, but with thine eyes ever fixed upon the Highest, press forward on the path of destiny, until the outward becomes the inward, and the discordant notes of nature blend in one great Amen.

Your friends greet you in the name of the Universal.

THE SCHOOL OF GIOTTO.

ANOTHER EXPERIENCE.

January, 1894.

DEAR FRIENDS,—I understand that you wish me to relate my experience after death, and I will do my best so to describe it that you may realize it to some degree.

With regard to my life on earth, it will be necessary to give you only those few particulars which had a direct influence on that experience.

I was in the prime of life when I passed over :—a man without close relationships, but with one very intimate friend. After twenty years of unbroken communion and fellowship, I discovered suddenly that my friend was false to me.

We were at that time separated by some hundreds of miles. I started off to confront

and upbraid him for this treachery when an
accident occurred, and in a few hours I was
dead. Death, what a misnomer ! To me it was
hardly a change ; I did not lose consciousness,
but stepped across the threshold and entered
the undiscovered country in which hitherto
I had not believed. There was to me no
sudden change, no violent displacement of
feeling or of circumstance ; but most gradually,
one by one, the old things gave place to the
new. The first change was this :—there
seemed to flow into my being a great stream
of health and of power. I breathed easily,
moved freely, and a sense of harmony with
my surroundings filled me. For a time it
was enough that I was alive ; mere sensation
was sufficient to satisfy me, and the knowledge
that there was life after death, even if it should
only persist for a time, was decidedly good.

You will naturally ask me here ; but what
were your experiences as to your environment ;

with what form, if any, were you clothed, and what were your new powers? I can only say that I was simply unaware of my surroundings and unconscious of myself. I mean that I did not ask myself where and what am I, but accepted all without question as one does generally in daily life, or in a dream. My sensations were not complex, but simple, and very gradually it dawned upon me that I had undergone a change.

After a period of pleasure in the strengthened natural powers of which I have spoken, there came to me the recollection of my friend and of his conduct to me. Then there sprang up a great sense of injustice and of hatred to him, and this was more powerful than I had felt in life.

At the same time I became aware, and this without surprise, that there was about me a number of men and women whose outward appearance made no conscious impression on me, but into whose inner being I seemed to look, and I found there like passions with my own ; hatred, desire for revenge, a calling for one's own rights at any cost to others ; a hungry, bitter, restless spirit ; this was in all hearts. "Welcome, brother, welcome," they all said; "there is no brotherhood so close as the brotherhood of hate."

There was something within me that responded at once and fully to this greeting; but no sooner had I done so, than a great darkness enveloped me. I lost consciousness, and a feeling akin to faintness took possession of me. How long I remained in this state I know not, but when I awoke it was to find myself still in darkness, a darkness that was now and again broken by flashes of light, revealing to me hidden shapes and fantastic forms that filled one's soul with thoughts of cruelty, or savage, revengeful fierceness. Yet I knew well that I did not really see these forms; I was aware that they were only as the distorted images of a dream, but the suffering and the horror were great. Harsh and terrifying sounds filled my senses and I cried aloud for some way of escape. Nearer and nearer came the figures, and louder and louder were the discordant noises, but just as they became unbearable there was a sudden lull, and again my senses forsook me.

Many times did this experience recur; and while I am obliged to describe it as if it were physical, it was not so, but in my inner self alone. Vainly I questioned myself as to why I thus suffered, and how I could escape. Is it because I cannot forgive the injustice, the deception of my friend? Yet if so, how was I to alter my mind towards him? Could I really forgive, truly and inwardly, just to escape suffering? I felt it to be impossible.

After a while a thought arose within me, which came like a blessed draught of water in

the desert. Give up this striving after a way
of thinking and of being, and let yourself go;
let nature do as she will; struggle no more to
think and experience in the old ways, let her
lead you in new paths. Once more my senses
sank in oblivion, and when again I became
conscious a sense of peace was within me,
though it was a peace rooted in sadness.

These alternations of feeling occurred again
and again in the same order; the terrors, the
soul-conflict, the temporary oblivion, the peaceful thought; yet ever increasing in intensity;
both the anguish and the peace being deeper.
Finally, after what may have been a day or a
thousand years, a change came. Consciously
I went over the whole of my earthly life,
especially in relation to my friend; but while
the circumstances passed before my mental
vision more clearly than when I had first lived
through them, the inner life was unrolled before
me in quite a different aspect.

I saw to my bitter mortification that through all it was I that had been in the wrong. I do not mean that my friend had not committed the act of treachery, nor yet that I was wrong in calling it treachery, but that the spirit in which I myself had lived had been altogether a wrong one. In the past I had thought that if the action were correct—moral, and the thoughts of the heart in accordance therewith, that was sufficient. Of the hidden springs of the spirit, the fountain that had sent up the waters, I had known nothing. All my life, I saw, had sprung from self, and returned to it again; therefore its limitations were so great, its form so puny and fruitless; it was a dead thing. What mattered it that another did or did not certain things; that was not the question, but what am I, and what is my relationship to others.

After this I became aware in some way of the present state of my friend's mind and feeling towards me and towards his action. I perceived that he was not at all sorry or ashamed of what he had done, but that rather he was relieved at my death. Also I saw that this last action was the outcome of many years, during which the inner reality of his affection had been eaten away, leaving only a hollow pretence.

Last of all there came to me a kind of review, a summing up, something in this way.

I understood, first, that my anguish was neither sent as a punishment, nor was it the outcome exactly of any special sin on my part. It was rather analogous to the pain of body caused by the twisting or distorting of a limb. My soul-vision had been distorted; I had seen the false rather than the true, and naturally I suffered. Next I saw that the special form which these experiences had taken was not so much because this one side of my life was more important than another, but because that incident had been so strongly impressed upon me just before death, therefore it became a kind of lesson book from which to learn these truths of life. So much for this first chapter of my history; I will now try to tell you how I began to live in reality.

About this time I saw that my friend was in a state of indecision as to his future action with regard to the very matter in which he had cheated me. One mode of action I saw, would bring him comfort and prosperity, the other, failure. I felt within myself the power to influence him either way. It was not difficult, however, for me to choose the right one, but when I did so, and he acted upon my suggestion, there came to me, not the peace that I expected, but a new tide of anguish. The crowd of embittered spirits who had welcomed me before, now turned from me, and, in awful loneliness, I lived apart in a desert land. Hungry and thirsty, my soul fainted within

me; yet underneath I was conscious of the
stirrings of a new life, which I felt was my
true one; and a voice said to me: "If you
would bear the sins of your brother, you must
be willing to bear the suffering which would
otherwise have been his."

After this I suddenly found myself back on
earth, approaching the house of my friend.
The old senses were again in use. I saw the
houses and the people; I heard the sounds in
the streets, but at once I recognized the fact
that these sights and sounds were what I had
heard and seen before my death : this was only
a vision, a memory ; all, all was unsubstantial
and shadowy, and again a great horror seized me.

After a while I returned (if I may so
express it) to this world, and those who had
previously turned from me now pressed eagerly
round enquiring as to the result of my visit
to my friend. "Are you avenged"? they
said ; "does he suffer for his sin"?

A strange feeling of pity filled my soul, as I looked into their hungry and miserable faces. "I am avenged," I said; "all my suffering has been made up for, and I am repaid a thousandfold." "How is that, tell us," they cried. "Simply by the old sense of hatred having died completely out of my being," I replied; "I have seen life from a new standpoint. No longer the centre of my own universe, all around has taken its proper place, and for past experiences I am only and simply glad whatever those experiences have been." "Fool!" they exclaimed, "then we cast you out of our brotherhood with all its advantages, and never again shall you have power to return to earth." "I shall go to my appointed place, wherever that may be," I said, and at that moment I became conscious of others round me whose bright, smiling, and loving looks were a great contrast to the others, whose faces began to grow dim, and gradually disappeared from my vision.

I then understood that sight was not like
the old physical vision, but that I could only
see what was really connected with my true
being, and that rays of soul-vision came to me
through the atmosphere of soul-character,
instead of through the atmosphere of earth.
For some time this sight of love and purity
was all that I perceived ; no intercourse could
I hold with them except by looks.

I quite despair, dear friends, of making
you know at all adequately the glory and joy
of the period that now commenced. Nothing
perhaps more surprised me than the great
variety of my experiences. Whenever I had,
during my earthly life, thought it possible that
there might be a future one, I had always
imagined it stationary ; a kind of blissful rest.
But how varied is the reality, and how far
removed from my old idea was my real life.
I now understood fully that I had cast off my
earthly body, and had one that was different ;

yet not so opposed as to be unfamiliar. I had not known hunger or fatigue; for those bodily needs and the functions that satisfied them were replaced by the needs and functions of the heart—of the emotional side of one's nature. All desires seemed to spring from the affections: love thirsted and was satisfied, hatred hungered, but was now dying of starvation: the wish to hold intercourse with others, and the longing to help them, blossomed into the power to will and to do.

After these feelings were satisfied, there came a sense of peaceful rest, akin to bodily slumber, and then again I would awaken to fresh desires.

At this time I entered into a special friendship with one to whom I was greatly attracted. I had no power to question him as to who he was or had been; but gradually, as a flower unfolds, his character unfolded itself before me. I saw in him what a true friend could be, and from that learned how faulty and pitiful my own friendship had been.

You may perhaps think I dwell too much on this subject; but the reason I do so is that these first experiences of mine were so closely connected with it. The ruling passion was not only strong in death, but it seems to be the impetus which drove me into this life, and determined its earlier course. Later on, earthly things faded, and I grew used to my new powers, but those it would be much more difficult to describe.

You will remember that I had been an unbeliever, and even after I passed over I thought the life here might be a kind of mechanical continuance of the other; like a top that goes on spinning after the hand that has set it going is removed. Now I saw that it was an independent, high and beautiful reality.

I must speak a little more of this friend, to

whom I was attracted by the mingled strength and sweetness which shone in his countenance. Without words we held communion, and I made known to him my past history. As I did this there came to me from him in response a growing sense of my own deficiencies, with a gradual, but complete dying out of all bitterness or animosity towards my friend. Thus the last wound was healed, and undisturbed by conflicting feelings, I was able to turn my face towards the future. "I, too," said he, "have known the bitterness of treachery; and more, the failure of the nearest to enter into my deepest self: but only thus can we know what true brotherhood is. Also, I myself sometimes failed in sympathy with planes of feeling other than my own." It was also through this true friend that I have had visions of another life, a higher one beyond even this; and these visions have at once strengthened me, and added greatly to my joy.

After some time of happy fellowship, new
desires sprang up within me. I wished, if
possible, to give as well as receive. You may
now return to those you saw first, I was told,
and help them to distinguish the true from the
false ; but it will be a painful task. I replied,
that I was willing to undertake it, and soon
I understood what is meant by the descent
into hell.

He descended into hell; the third day He
rose again. How very true that old creed is,
if we view it in a larger way as speaking of
Man and his universal experience !

I believe in One, the everliving Father, and
in His Son, Jesus Christ,—(Man) who is con-
ceived of the Holy Ghost, born of the Virgin.
He suffers, dies, and rises again ; he ascends
into heaven, and from there judges both the
living and the dead. Happy are we if when
our individual turn comes to descend into hell
we know that even in the bed of hell the

Higher One is with us. How shall I explain to you the state of these souls in prison! The pain arises chiefly from this: The body is cast off, but while the man still dwells on the earthly plane he cannot use his new powers, therefore the limitations of his nature are so great, he is so straitly shut up in himself that it is like a conscious death; he cannot do the old things and is ignorant of the new; he is in the chrysalis state of the psyche. My part was to suffer with them, while knowing that there was a new and better way, and by my sympathy, lead them to believe in it. I could now say, " Take up thy bed and walk "; and they, having learned to believe in me, could make the effort and find it possible to obey.

Here, no counsel, no reasoning can be apart from yourself. You cannot say to another: Do this, believe that, unless at the same time you do it for them yourself; otherwise they would neither hear nor understand.

This state of sin-bearing, of mediatorship, lasted what seemed to me a life time; but a deeply inwrought sense of willingness upheld me, and would have done so even if the furnace had been heated seven times.

You may think that the trials and experiences through which I have passed should rather have been given to my false friend than to myself, but this would be to take a superficial view. The "eye for an eye " methods have been condemned by all who think deeply. I needed a certain teaching, a special training, and this training which was begun on earth, was carried out and completed here. Or at least so far completed that I was made fit for a new life, on which I have now entered. The suffering was enlightening and ennobling, now the joy is pure and unspeakable; old things are indeed passed away and behold all things are made new.

THE STORY OF THE GLACIER.

Received at the foot of the Morteratsch Glacier, Pontresina.
June, 1890.

ONCE upon a time, long, long ago, when the dear Lord dwelt alone upon the earth, and man was not yet created,—there was a Glacier. The head of the Glacier was in the skies, and its feet were in the valley, and the valley was all stony and bare, no tree, nor flower grew there, for there was no water.

Now in the morning, and in the evening, the dear Lord walked in that valley, and when He came the Glacier put a veil of gold upon its head, and the Glacier was happy.

Now as years went on the Lord God was lonely ; therefore He made man that He might pour out His love upon him, and man filled the earth and cultivated it ; but none dwelt in the

valley at the foot of the Glacier, for there was
no water there. And it came to pass that the
Glacier was unhappy. One morning he said to
the dear Lord : " My master, would that I were
of some use in this world of Thine ; would that
man could dwell under my shade, and that the
valley might smile under my glance ! " The
Lord said : " If thou art willing to suffer, it
shall be so." And the Lord smiled upon the
Glacier, and when He smiled, a sharp pang
went through the heart of the Glacier, sharper
than a sword-thrust in the bosom of a tender
woman. The Glacier would not cry out, but
bore the anguish in silence. And in a moment
its heart was rent asunder, and from it flowed a
mighty stream of living water. And the water
laughed and sang, and leaped down into the
valley, pouring forth its life-giving stream. It
came to pass, in course of time, that trees and
flowers sprang up there, and man came and
planted the corn and vine, and little children

looked up into the face of the Glacier and smiled, and the Glacier was happy.

Now there stood by the Glacier, One—and he said to the Lord, "My Father, why is it permitted to the glacier to have this divine joy of suffering, while to me, thy Son, it is not permitted?" And the Lord said, "My Son, I have done all things well," and the Son bowed his head and worshipped.

THE STORY OF THE TREE.

Received June, 1892.

A LONG time ago, there lived in the forest a Tree, and its branches were stunted and gnarled, and all its leaves mal-formed and jagged. And the Tree said, "Why is this, surely the One that planted me ought to have known better. I am of no good to man or beast." At that moment a woodman came into the forest, and passing by all the goodly, well-shaped trees, saying, " They will not serve my purpose,"—came where the ragged, old Tree lifted up its misshapen branches to the sun. Said he, " Why this is the very thing ; this will serve my purpose well." With that he called his fellows, and cut it down. Lo ! when it had been sawn asunder, the most exquisite veins of beauty were found running through the heart of it, and the tracing was more lovely than any artist could have fashioned, and of it were made many beautiful articles of use and ornament for the King's Palace.

APPENDIX.

APPENDIX.

So many references have been made in the foregoing to dimensions and dimensional laws, that the following, which was received in 1891, may be of some help to the reader :—

DEAR FRIEND,—I am told you have been interested in the fourth dimension. There *is* a fourth dimension, which you can easily understand, though you have not attained to it yet. Beside the line, the square, and the cube, there is something which represents what you might call the inter-penetrative sphere. You have motion forward, upward, across; but in the future there will also be motion through. At present one body has to move out of the way of another, but *then* they will just inter-penetrate.

Now, as you know, no two bodies touch ; but then, not only would solid (so called) pass through solid by the separation of each molecule, but also there would be a fusion of molecules and a separation again when desired. This is inter-sphericity, or inter-penetration of spheres.

This fourth dimension, only guessed at by you, is our first, the other three fall from us as crude and imperfect. To understand this more easily, think of the simile used of the man who could only walk in two dimensions. *You* can walk in three, but in the future there will be four—up, down, across, through.

I think a symbol to be added to the line, the square, and the cube might be this : a hollow sphere, with other hollow and smaller spheres enclosed within it, something like the balls within balls cut by the Chinese. These spheres must be thought of as composed of a kind of elastic fluid ; the larger spheres by compression passable through the smaller, and the smaller by expansion passable through the larger. Thus each sphere can be within or without the others.

Now to leave the symbol and return to the new power which it represents: the solid can become fluid, pass through the solid (which is for the time also fluid) and then resume its first form.

This power, when perfected, would give man absolute power of progression in every direction and in every part of the universe. He could pass through the heart of mountains, or could rise into the atmosphere to any height by altering, as it were, his own density, and the density of his path ; nothing would prove a hindrance.

Next as to the fifth dimension. Here I shall have more difficulty.

You have been already taught that your world and ours are not like two globes side by side and independent of each other, but as a spirit inhabits a body, so our world inhabits yours. To pass from yours to ours requires the violent change of death to the body (at least, in most cases). You cannot pass to us, nor we to you, but in very exceptional and partial ways. But there will be a time when the limits of this visible world will be its limits no longer, and from the seen to the unseen the human being will be able to pass with the greatest rapidity and ease. The Son of Man attained to this power for a time, and in a limited degree, and there have been prophecies and hints of it at different times ; but in future, as easily as your thought passes from place to place, so will you, or those who come after you.

Let us call the fourth dimension inter-progression, then the fifth might be called trans-progression. From sphere to sphere, from star to star, and from star to sun shall the children of men wander at free will. (I do not mean visible stars, but I mean the great Unseen.) Our first and rudimentary state it would be, into which you would pass. This, perhaps, you will have understood.

As men rise from dimension to dimension their powers are changed and increased in many ways. It is not simply an added power of progression, but an opening ot new faculties in many directions.   There are on our side beings who come over so undeveloped in any higher part of them, that all to which they can attain is the power of passing from place to place without let or hindrance, a kind of animal life.   Some linger in the atmosphere of your world, seeking to feed their feeble earth-bound souls, and it is from this class that most physical manifestations are obtained, the link that binds their lower nature to earth not being yet broken.

These dimensional laws begin very low down in the purely physical, and gradually rise as the powers of the being are developed and increased.   There is no sharp division, as you know, between the physical and psychical ; psychical and spiritual ; and again between spiritual and that higher state still which you call Divine.

The sixth dimension begins to enter upon higher ground, yet I think you can follow a little farther.   The first five have to do with what we may call *space;* the next series has to do more directly with what you call *time.*

In the first time-dimension the experience of the being is that he is no longer limited by time in the way you are ; time is not either long or short ; a lifetime may be lived through in a moment, or a moment may extend to a lifetime ; one day is with Him as a thousand years, or a thousand years as one day.

Do I need to perform any action ? I am not bound or hampered by time. So the Master produced the wheaten bread in a moment, or restored the wasted tissues of the human frame in a few brief seconds ; while on other occasions the power seemed to fail Him, and He cried, "I have a work to do, and how am I straitened until it be accomplished." This dimension we only partly enter into, but there are higher spirits to whom it is the normal state.

Next the seventh or second time-dimension. In this the being advances a stage farther ; here the limitations of time fall from him more completely than before ; for him, indeed, time may be said to have no existence. The past (or what has been called past) to Him is the same as the present, and only the future lies still closed to Him ; something of the spirit and power of the Eternal I AM is within him, and he approaches still more nearly the Divine.

Your memory is limited to those ineffaceable marks on the rock of your being made at some period by the waves of your conscious life.

But to him this is not so ; all things lie within his memory. More than that, they can in a real manner unfold themselves before him at his will. This power adds largely to the joy of those higher spheres in which he dwells.

This power was hinted at by the Master when He said, " Before Abraham was, I am."

After the time-dimensions come those that belong more directly to the human will, its powers and its limitations.

.

www.ingramcontent.com/pod-product-compliance
Lightning Source LLC
Chambersburg PA
CBHW020534270326
41927CB00006B/575